"This book is essential, invaluable, and necessary for any screenwriter wanting to make it in the competitive buyer's world. Kathie Fong Yoneda gives the insider's view in a kind, encouraging, insightful way. A fascinating read into how things really work and what the writer can do, without compromising a vision."
— Dr. Linda S. Seger, Script Consultant and Author
Making A Good Script Great, Creating Unforgettable Characters, Making A Good Writer Great

"If you haven't had a chance to sit in on one of Kathie's workshops as I have, or to watch her demonstrate the magic of a great pitch, here's your opportunity to experience the insight, guidance, and support she gives to those pursuing a career in screenwriting. With *The Script-Selling Game*, she's managed to bring all her wisdom and humanity into this terrific book."
— Michael Hauge
Author, *Writing Screenplays That Sell*

"Kathie lights a fire under you and then walks you through it."
— Jeff Arch, Screenwriter, *Sleepless in Seattle*

"Super-concise, systematic, real-world advice on the practical aspects of screenwriting and mastering Hollywood from a professional. Kathie's book will save you time, embarrassment, and frustration, and will give you an extra edge in taking on the studio system."
— Christopher Vogler, Story Consultant and Author
The Writer's Journey

"From the basics to the more complicated, Kathie Fong Yoneda answers all the questions most screenwriters ask, and then some. Her knowledge is sweeping, her love of the business is palpable, and her respect for her audience is readily apparent. This is the best way to get advice: from someone who knows and cares."
— Donie A. Nelson, Career Strategies for Writers

"Kathie Fong Yoneda brings clarity and common sense to a world seemingly designed to intimidate."
— Ron Mardigan, Professor, USC School of Cinema & Television, former Senior VP of the William Morris Agency

"Kathie Fong Yoneda absolutely knows about what she writes! Following her advice could make a material difference in ultimately getting your script purchased and produced."

> — Richard A. Shepherd, Partner at The Artists
> Agency; former Head of Production at MGM;
> Producer, *Breakfast at Tiffany's, Twelve Angry Men*

"Written by an industry insider, whose valuable experience both reading and recommending scripts has resulted in successfully produced projects. Kathie's book accurately shows you what the studios are looking for."

> — Marshall Coben, VP, Paramount Pictures
> Television Longform

"This book may be the ultimate rocket fuel to launch your writing career in Hollywood."

> — Tess Gerritsen, Screenwriter, *Adrift*;
> Novelist, *Harvest, Gravity, The Surgeon*

"*The Script-Selling Game* is a straight-forward journey into what it takes to get your script noticed by the decision-makers in Hollywood. This book offers screenwriters a healthy and refreshing collection of advice full of amazing insights that would otherwise take many years and mistakes to learn. If you truly want to know how the film business works and make inroads with your screenwriting career, this is the book to take you there."

> — John Johnson, American Screenwriters Association

"Board games come with a set of rules. A car comes with an owner's manual. Screenwriting should come with this book. Yoneda succeeds in writing a comprehensive cross between a rule book and a manual that every beginning screenwriter would be well-advised to read."

> — Jeffrey M. Somogyi, *New York Screenwriter*

"Kathie offers real insights and great practical advice on the craft as well as the business of writing. *The Script-Selling Game* is like having Kathie as your own personal teacher, coach, and mentor."

> — Scott Burnell, Chairman
> StoryBoard Development Group

MICHAEL WIESE PRODUCTIONS
www.mwp.com

Since 1981, Michael Wiese Productions has been dedicated to providing novice and seasoned filmmakers with vital information on all aspects of filmmaking and videomaking. We have published more than 50 books, used in over 500 film schools worldwide.

Our authors are successful industry professionals — they believe that the more knowledge and experience they share with others, the more high-quality films will be made. That's why they spend countless hours writing about the hard stuff: budgeting, financing, directing, marketing, and distribution. Many of our authors, including myself, are often invited to conduct filmmaking seminars around the world.

We truly hope that our publications, seminars, and consulting services will empower you to create enduring films that will last for generations to come.

We're here to help. Let us hear from you.

Sincerely,

Michael Wiese
Publisher, Filmmaker

THE SCRIPT-SELLING GAME

A Hollywood Insider's Look at Getting Your Script Sold and Produced

by
Kathie Fong Yoneda

Published by Michael Wiese Productions
11288 Ventura Blvd., Suite 621
Studio City, CA 91604
tel. (818) 379-8799
fax (818) 986-3408
mw@mwp.com
www.mwp.com

Cover Design: Objects of Design
Book Layout: Gina Mansfield
Editor: Brett Jay Markel

Printed by McNaughton & Gunn, Inc., Saline, Michigan
Manufactured in the United States of America

©2002 Kathie Fong Yoneda

"Academy Award" and "Oscar" are the registered trademarks and service marks of the Academy of Motion Picture Arts and Sciences.

ISBN 0-941188-44-2

Library of Congress Cataloging-in-Publication Data

Yoneda, Kathie Fong, 1946–
    The script-selling game: a Hollywood insider's look at getting your script
    sold and produced/ by Kathie Fong Yoneda.
      p. cm.
    ISBN 0-941188-44-2
  1. Motion picture authorship. I. Title.

PN1996 .Y58 2002
808.2'3--dc21   2002003462

To Denny,
whose unconditional love and patience
amazes and inspires me

TABLE OF CONTENTS

PART IV – THINKING BEYOND THE SCRIPT: THE ONGOING WORK OF A WRITER TO HIS WORK AND RELATIONSHIPS

PREFACE

By Pamela Wallace, Writer-Producer
(Academy Award Co-Winner, Best Writing, Screenplay Written
Directly for the Screen, Witness, *1985)*

When I began my screenwriting career, I knew very little about the craft of writing, and even less about how the movie business actually works. I had almost no contacts in the business, so there was no trusted friend or knowledgeable insider I could ask questions of. It would have helped enormously to have someone I could turn to when I was confused or uncertain. Someone who could help me see what I was doing right or wrong. Who could explain this crazy business to me. And help me understand what I needed to do to make my dream of becoming a professional screenwriter come true.

Through trial and error, and often painful experience, I gradually learned the craft of screenwriting. And, even more critically, came to understand the business side of the film industry. Because it does not matter if you write the greatest screenplay ever, if it is not the kind of thing the filmmakers are buying. If only I had had a resource like this book, it would have made my learning curve an awful lot quicker and easier.

Kathie Fong Yoneda, a story analyst/development specialist with an impressive background in the film business, is the trusted friend and knowledgeable insider every aspiring writer needs. Story analysts are usually the first to read your script and recommend it or pass on it. Kathie is one of those people who decides which scripts reach the people who are in a position to buy them. Her judgment is not only trusted and respected by those people, it is often the determining factor in whether or not a script is accepted or rejected.

In this insightful and informative book — filled with the wisdom, advice, and critical information that only someone with her experience could possess — you'll learn the essentials to making it past gatekeepers (like Kathie, herself!) who determine if your script is worthy of serious consideration. In this ultimate insider's guide to Hollywood, Kathie tells you:

- The qualities a script *must* have to be seriously considered by a studio or a production company

- How the process works once your script disappears into the Black Hole that is the studio system

- The fatal errors to avoid at all costs

She offers practical techniques to make your writing shine and stand out. In that respect, and in so many others, this creative and commercial guide stands alone.

When I read this book, I assumed I pretty much already knew this stuff. Instead, I discovered so many things I did not know or had lost sight of. For example, the chapter on pitching has changed the way I handle pitch meetings. I re-read it before every meeting, to remind myself exactly how to impress the prospective buyer.

A practical guide to the ins and outs of an exciting but challenging arena, this book is of equal value to experienced writers who want to hone their craft and to new writers tackling their first script. It is, in short, the writer's best friend, and a vital aid in a highly competitive and potentially lucrative business.

I have been extremely fortunate to have had Kathie's insightful advice and constructive criticism on my screenplays. She has been a valued mentor to me. Now, through this wonderful book, she can be your mentor, as well.

ACKNOWLEDGMENTS

It seems that nearly everyone I meet knows someone who is writing a book or a script that deserves to be a theatrical or television movie. The public eagerly reads about the multi-million dollar deals in Tinseltown and thousands of people pursue Hollywood's brass ring.

The truth with all such pursuits is that some will succeed and will, indeed, capture the dream of a career in film and television, but many others will not. Sometimes what is stopping a screenwriter is not his or her talent, but the lack of knowledge about the industry and how it works.* I hope this book can help demystify the industry for you.

For four years I wrote a popular monthly column on the "Biz," focusing mostly on screenwriting and development. I had a chance to meet many readers of my work at conferences and seminars, some of whom would show me the tattered copies of my columns they had put in a notebook or folder — all of them pleading with me to publish them in a book.

After much procrastination and prodding and with a lot of encouragement and support, this book is the final result. But as I found out, it was not enough to simply reprint my columns. For a change, I found myself on the same side of the desk as the writers... conquering writer's block, researching and updating

---

*This is the last time you will read the phrases "his or her" or "he or she"; from this point on, I will use one or the other pronoun and assume you understand that at any single time, either sex could apply.

material, and juggling my work and my life as the manuscript deadline approached.

Through this journey I realized, with great clarity, just how fortunate I have been to have had the friendship and support of so many people throughout my career.

I learned the meaning of hard work and integrity from my former boss, Richard A. Shepherd, who gave me my first opportunity by opening a door and reminding me that it was up to me to do my best once I was inside.

I embraced the importance of sharing and giving from a special "web" of industry consultants: Linda Seger, Pamela Jaye Smith, Donie Nelson, Chris Vogler, and Carolyn Miller, while I have appreciated the enduring friendship of my dear gal-pals, Pam Wallace and Madeline DiMaggio, who have kept me going even when I cursed this crazy business.

The late Steve Lester, Meera Lester, and John Johnson have shown me the vision and the dedication it takes to help others realize their dreams through their conference, *Selling to Hollywood*, while Pierre Challain and Jean-Michel Albert and the members of Thot Fiction have inspired me with their passion for connecting the world through film.

Even before I knew that Hollywood would be my destiny, I have had the love and the support of my Mom and Dad and the heart-felt treasure of tears and laughter from my sisters, Dana, 'trice, and Laureen.

To Michael Wiese, Ken Lee, and B. J. Markel: Thank you for believing in me and making my words sound even better! To Scott Baillie: Thanks for helping me to "make the connection." To Jan Stiles, who edited my original columns and was always so encouraging. And to Robin Rindner: Thank you for the invaluable lessons on "merge," "page numbering," and "copying to disc."

Kathie Fong Yoneda
April, 2002

PART I – IN THE BEGINNING...

CHAPTER 1

DEVELOPING SCRIPT IDEAS

One of my clients sent me her screenplay, a murder mystery which was a real page-turner and a major leap forward from her first two scripts. When I asked her for the genesis of this intriguing effort, she excitedly replied, "I found out my husband was having an affair, and I wanted to kill him, but my therapist told me to find another way to let out my feelings, so I killed him in my script!" Who'd have thought of developing a great film idea through therapy?

The world has been making movies for well over a hundred years now. And instead of stand-alone theaters in large cities, films can now be seen on television, cable, video, DVD, and even online. There are 24-hour stores where you can rent a movie, even at 3:00 in the morning, or you can simply take your laptop or DVD player with you on a plane or in your camper.

With all these available outlets comes another problem: creating and developing the ideas for the movie-hungry masses. Despite the public's ever-growing hunger for films, the number of movies produced every year in the United States for theatrical release has remained relatively the same — just a little over 300 motion pictures a year. Most of the output of films in Western Europe has also remained the same. Surprisingly, such countries as India and China have actually increased their output of movies.

When asked why more movies are not made, I can only tell you that moviemaking is big business, and before a studio is going to spend millions of dollars on a film, its executives want to hedge their bets. Hollywood has found that the best way to do that is to nurture a project from the very beginning. One Hollywood notable was quoted as saying that "In Hollywood... the idea is king." I would like to modify that statement slightly. In actuality, it is the *story* that is king.

Ideas are not even copyrightable, so it is hard to "own" or "claim" an idea. An idea is only a thought unless you build a viable story around it, populating it with characters who are caught up in a physical and/or emotional dilemma, giving them dialogue that says something funny, profound, or meaningful, and most of all, providing the audience with a way to be touched and entertained.

WHERE DO IDEAS COME FROM?
Ideas for movies come from the same sources as all good storytelling — from experiences, both real and imagined. Starting with the cavemen who boasted of their latest hunt, being lost in the wilderness, or saving their families from a rock slide, right on up to blockbusters like *Harry Potter and the Sorcerer's Stone, Titanic, Shrek, Dances With Wolves,* or *Jurassic Park*, good storytelling only

2

differs in the format. The cavemen used their rudimentary form of language and supplemented their "history" with drawings on the walls of their cave dwellings. Luckily, we have advanced and can now use our computers to create novels and scripts.

Stories can emanate from past experiences, fashioned around historical events or placed in another era to show us the difficulties of the time. They can also spring from our imagined experiences as we wonder about what will happen in the future. A majority of the stories come from our present experience, from what is going on in our world as we speak. What successful film stories seem to share — no matter whether they are set in the past, the future, or the present — is the "human experience."

High Concept/Low or Soft Concept?

Writers are always asking me whether they should write a movie based on an idea that is "high concept" or "low/soft concept." **High concept** usually means that the central story of the film can be easily summarized and will appeal to a larger audience. In other words, loosely translated, high concept movies are generally thought to be more commercial and thus, may bring in more moviegoers (translation: more money) to the theaters.

Low or soft concept is usually applied to a film that may focus on a more complex set of life circumstances or around a more specific issue — both of which can limit the number of people who might be interested in viewing the film.

However, as we all know, a "more commercial" movie is not always a "better" one. In mid-February, the motion picture industry holds its collective breath as the nominations are announced for the Academy Awards. It should come as no surprise that most of the motion pictures nominated do not seem to fall into the big-budget, "more commercial" films that have grossed $200 million or more globally. Instead, most of the Best Picture nominations seem to favor those "smaller" special films, many of which were made for less than one-tenth the budget of their high-concept cousins.

In general, high concept can usually be defined as having a more "plot-driven" focus, while a low- or soft-concept project is usually more "character-driven." But there are exceptions to every rule and every generalization. Motion pictures like *Titanic, Saving Private Ryan,* and *The Sixth Sense* succeeded because they found a successful balance and were both plot- and character-driven.

ADAPTATIONS

Other sources for movies are novels, myths, legends, the Bible, magazine articles, plays, current events, and fairy tales. Whether a film is based on a *New York Times* best-selling novel, taken from a classic tale from Shakespeare, or surfaces as an updated version of the familiar fairy tale, *Cinderella*, many screenwriters find inspiration in literature and stories of yore.

But adapting a project, especially based on written material that is not old enough to be in public domain, can be somewhat tricky. If you want to adapt a best-selling novel into a screenplay, you will have to contact the publishing house to see if the film rights are available. If they are, you would be wise to contact an attorney who specializes in film rights to secure permission for you to adapt the novel. Surprisingly, some novelists (usually those whose books are not currently on the best-seller lists) have been known to allow a lucky screenwriter to option the rights to a script adaptation of their novel for as little as one dollar!

But anyone wishing to write a script based on already-published material should be warned: Studios will not touch a project if the writer has not secured the rights. The reason is obvious: A project without rights would be opening them up to a major lawsuit.

You should also tread carefully if you wish to base your project on a current event. While much of what we read in the newspapers or see on CNN can be considered public domain, you would be wise to check with an attorney, especially if you plan to focus on specific persons who are key figures in the event. While some people may not mind having a film based on their heroics or a tragic event in their lives, others may find it an invasion of privacy.

If you have tried, without much success, to secure the rights to individuals connected to a current event, you may want to consider fictionalizing the story by creating your own characters, using a different perspective, and/or providing an unusual twist that would make your story more unique and possibly more dramatic.

WHAT IF...?

The best advice I can offer to get a writer started on a new idea is to take the phrase, "What if...?" and fill in the rest of the sentence. The main reason most people enjoy going to the movies is that once we are seated in that darkened theater, we are hoping to be magically transported. Movies probe into our emotions, fears, and imagination. And in the process, they sometimes serve as "wish fulfillment" (what if?) as we find ourselves at the controls of Apollo 13 with Tom Hanks or next to Russell Crowe fighting hungry lions and demented emperors in the Roman Coliseum.

Here are examples of how some popular movies might have been born if their creators had started out with the words, "What if...?":

- What if... a struggling U.S. reporter in Rome stumbled upon a royal Princess who was incognito and wanted to see what "real life" was like? (*Roman Holiday*)

- What if... a rag-tag group of unemployed Brits threw caution to the wind and decided to "bare-it-all" in order to earn some money, as well as take back their self-respect? (*The Full Monty*)

- What if... a young boy, worried about his lonely widowed father, called into a national talk show for advice? (*Sleepless in Seattle*)

- What if... a Roman soldier who has lost his family finds a way to exact revenge on a cruel emperor by becoming a crowd-pleasing gladiator? (*Gladiator*)

Many entertaining films (be they high or low/soft concept) are often based on one of two situations:

- Taking an ordinary person and putting him in an extraordinary set of circumstances (*It Could Happen to You, Legally Blonde, Cast Away, Tootsie*).

- Taking an extraordinary person and putting him in an ordinary set of circumstances (*E.T. the Extra-Terrestrial, Rainman, Artificial Intelligence: A.I., Forrest Gump*).

What Is Story?

Once you have found an idea or several ideas to incorporate into your script, you will need a framework for your story. But what comprises a story? When I asked this question at a recent writers conference, most respondents quickly answered that story is "plot." While the plot is certainly one of the key aspects of a successful story, it is not the only element.

In general, a successful film story consists of the following:

- **Plot** — the situation, dilemma, or series of challenges in which the characters find themselves

- **People** — whose jobs are to carry out the plot

- Their **Surroundings** — their work, city/locale, family, etc.

- **Tone** — a balanced and somewhat consistent blend of responses and emotions to the plot

While plot, people, and surroundings are more evident in constructing a story, it is tone that often helps to elevate a story, providing the more recognizable emotional triggers that will entice an audience.

Themes/Emotions

Many popular movies are based on themes that are connected to emotional situations and responses. From the beginning of the Greek and Roman myths to pop and hip-hop music, emotional responses have triggered creativity. Here are just a few examples of films which have benefited from strong emotionally-themed underpinnings:

- GREED — *Wall Street* and *Double Indemnity*

7

- REVENGE — *Ocean's 11* and *The Godfather* series

- SIBLING RIVALRY —*Whatever Happened to Baby Jane?*
  and *Twins*

- MISFORTUNE — The *Mad Max* series, *The Full Monty*,
  and *My Left Foot*

- PASSION — *Body Heat, First Knight*, and *Camelot*

- JEALOUSY — *Othello, O*, and *Ghost*

- REMORSE — *Unforgiven, In the Line of Fire*, and *My Life
  As A House*

There are dozens of other emotions and emotionally-charged situations that can serve to drive your characters and plot, thus transforming your idea into a fully-realized story. Referring to the tales that emanated from legends, folklore, or mythology can serve as a touchstone to ignite your own film or television project.

THE BLOCKBUSTER MOVIE

I wish I had a penny for each time an emerging writer said, "I want to write a blockbuster movie....Tell me how to write a blockbuster movie." No one has a magic formula for writing a blockbuster movie, but there are some elements that most successful blockbusters have in common:

- There must be broad audience appeal where the story can instantly "hook" a large portion of the movie-going public and is not offensive or demeaning to a significant segment of the audience.

8

• The overall story offers something out of the ordinary, something you are unlikely to see on television. (Television movies are often on limited budgets and are not likely to include expensive action sequences, complex special effects, or sweeping cinematography.)

• Most blockbusters seem to be rooted in the following genres: action (*The Terminator* series), fantasy (*Monsters, Inc.*), high-concept comedy (*Men in Black*), or a sweeping historical saga with tremendous scope (*Braveheart*). On occasion, a drama or a romance can become a blockbuster. (*Titanic* is one such example.)

• Most blockbusters seem to be loosely structured with a mythical underpinning that the audience immediately recognizes and embraces. (The *Star Wars* series and *The Godfather* series are two obvious examples.)

• The hero or heroine is someone the audience can easily relate to and sympathize with. The inclusion of such overwhelming sympathy for the protagonist is what is commonly called the **root-ability factor**. Anti-heroes rarely make for blockbusters, although some may argue that *The English Patient* is one of those exceptions.

• The protagonist must be pitted against either a set of circumstances that are nearly overwhelming or against a villain who seems to have everything in his favor. A protagonist cannot be heroic if the challenges she faces (be they human or otherwise) are not truly worthy of that victorious happy ending.

9

- The tone of the movie (even if it is a comedy) should be smart, but not intellectual. There is a difference between a character who is "intelligent" and one who is "intellectual." Audiences will get behind someone who may be intelligent but, because of misfortune, finds himself at the bottom of the heap. They rarely will cheer on a character who displays only his intellect and not his vulnerabilities or "humanness."

- Most blockbusters have a satisfying ending. This does not necessarily mean a traditional, happy ending, though happy endings are much more common. "Satisfying" can mean a bittersweet ending, wherein failure or tragic sacrifice is lightened by a sense of fulfillment. *Saving Private Ryan* and *Titanic* are two examples of a bittersweet, but fulfilling and appropriately satisfying ending.

- Above all, a blockbuster should tap into and portray people's fears or fantasies, giving them a chance (at least for two hours) to live in a world or in a situation they have only imagined.

If you check out the highest-grossing films of all times, more than half of the motion pictures listed will contain nearly all of the elements profiled above.

A REALITY CHECK
Although I have given you a list of elements that are common in blockbuster films, it is also important to realize that many of the movies on the highest-grossing list were not initially thought to be blockbusters by either the producers or the studios that were involved.

Twentieth Century Fox was surprised and overwhelmed when respondents at the previews of *Star Wars* gave such high marks and positive comments to what Fox's marketing department thought would be "a nice family-style, sci-fi movie" (actually, it is technically a science-fantasy). But when everyone from teenagers to baby boomers to grandparents gave the film some of the highest responses in history, Fox knew it had a potential hit on its hands. They quickly stepped up their marketing campaign and *Star Wars* has gone on to spawn one of the most successful franchises ever — without showing any signs of stopping.

One of the most talked-about success tales involves the film *Forrest Gump*. Warner Bros. originally had the film on their development slate, but did not have much faith in the project and made the decision to put it in **turnaround** (put up for sale, usually to another studio that is willing to pay for any costs incurred up to that point). A rival studio, Paramount Pictures, quickly recognized the potential for the project and paid Warner Bros. its costs. Paramount went on to make the movie and was happy to add another Best Picture Oscar to its display case, as well as a huge grin at the movie's then sixth place standing among the Top Ten highest-grossing films of all time.

The Full Monty is another example of a film whose grosses stunned its distributors and producers. The heartfelt tale of a group of unemployed, small-town Brits who regain their self-respect and the love of the town's citizens by "baring all" was made for less than $3 million, but was the most profitable film in 1997. It is what the industry humorously calls a **sleeper**, because its success was unexpected.

What *The Full Monty*, *Forrest Gump*, and *Star Wars* have in common (besides having grossed hundreds of millions of dollars at the box office) is that each of these projects has "heart." Their characters may have lived literally "light years" apart, but they all struggled with the need for respect and acceptance, and in their own way, gained the faith and the courage to prove themselves.

There have been many writers whose motion pictures contained many of the elements that are common in blockbusters, yet their films did not succeed. On the other hand, there have been movies that were initially considered "nice" or "small" or "quirky" which had something profound to say about the human condition, and in the process, captured the audience's hearts and pocketbooks! So when considering an idea for a film project, be aware that there is plenty of room for both commercial and independent-type films. The moral of this chapter is: Whatever your story/idea is, write it with passion and heart and not just thoughts of making money!

CHAPTER 2

PREPARING FOR THE BUSINESS SIDE
OF SCRIPTING

In addition to writing a sure-to-be-a-hit screenplay, an emerging screenwriter would be wise to also prepare himself for what is known as the "business side of scripting." When faced with the prospect of sending out your "baby" to potential agents, entertainment attorneys, studios, or production execs, do you know which persons in which positions can help you most? Do you know what kinds of budgetary limitations can play a role in whether your submission is a "recommend" or a "pass"? And are you aware of the role that the Writers Guild of America can play in your screenwriting career?

Knowing the answers to these questions can often put you and your projects one step ahead of the thousands of other eager scriptwriters who are also knocking anxiously on Hollywood's front gates.

KNOWING THE PLAYERS
The persons in charge of making decisions on which projects will be bought are collectively called the creative group. If you are targeting a production company or if a studio exec is anxious to hear about your newest project, you should definitely know who is part of this group and what its members do.

At the studios, **the creative group** consists of the head of the motion picture division, followed by the senior or executive vice presidents of production, the vice presidents of production, the directors of development (also referred to as creative execs), and the story editor. In a larger production company, you would have the producer (who is the principal owner), followed by either a senior vice president or vice president of production, a director of development and, occasionally, a story editor.

Where novice writers often make a mistake is targeting the "higher-ups." In other words, they send their query letters or screenplays to the head of the motion picture division or the senior executives. If you have limited experience as a screenwriter, the better bet is to focus on the directors of development or the story editors.

The senior executives will usually be dealing with the established writers, acting talent, and producers. The directors of development and the story editors (who aspire to be senior executives or heads of studios or production companies) are more willing to search for and find new talent to prove themselves. In fact, discovering a new writer helps their own careers. It not only shows their bosses that they have uncommon initiative, but also proves that they are willing to work harder to identify the talent that is necessary to "regenerate" the industry every few years. Eager to make a name for themselves, the execs on the lower rungs of the executive ladder are usually more eager ("hungrier") and tend to be risk-takers.

Here's just a partial list of the creative group's responsibilities that directly affect a writer:

- Acquiring material which can be developed into motion pictures. The group reads scripts, treatments, plays, unpublished manuscripts, books, and news articles.

- Looking for new writing talent, mostly to fill any open writing assignments for an in-house idea or to rewrite or polish an existing project which requires a new writer. Besides reading scripts of new clients submitted by agents, the creative group also reads the scripts of the finalists from some of the major screenplay competitions and "screens" (views) short films which are written and directed by film-school students.

- Finding projects by taking pitch meetings with writers whose work they have read, hoping to get an early edge on a new script.

WOOING THE AGENCIES AND THE PRODUCTION COMPANIES
Almost every emerging scriptwriter (and especially those who live outside of the immediate Southern California or New York City areas) would love to send her material to an agent for possible representation. In discussing the art of doing business with agents, several screenwriters told me about their strategies for "wooing" the agencies and the production companies.

If you have the time, patience, and money, try calling some of the mid-level and smaller agencies. If you are unable to talk directly with an agent, you might try talking with his assistant. This approach may sound like a long shot, but many a successful writer has gotten a "break" from an assistant who was eager to prove himself as "agent material" to his boss by finding new talent on his own.

One playwright offered to give an agent two free tickets to his play which he had recently adapted into a script. When the assistant got on the line to tell the playwright that the agent had declined his offer, the playwright asked the assistant to be his guest. The result? The assistant not only enjoyed the play, but asked to see the writer's screenplay adaptation and got his boss to read it. The agent ended up representing the playwright-cum-screenwriter. That assistant is now an agent at one of the larger agencies.

The same has also proven to work when it comes to assistants at production companies, since most assistants aspire to be development executives and producers. On a whim, an emerging screenwriter called the production company that had sent her a generic rejection letter. She asked to speak to the person who had signed the letter. It turned out to be the assistant to the producer. The writer asked him for some advice on the best way to get her material read, and the assistant told her, "It is who you know...." They chatted a little more about how hard it was to break into the business and the writer asked if the assistant would consider reading her script in exchange for a cup of coffee. The assistant took a chance; they met at a West Hollywood coffee café. Today the assistant is a director of development at the same production company because he took that chance. He read the script, got his boss to read it; he optioned it and recommended the writer to an agent friend who ended up representing her — all because she took some time to cultivate a relationship with the assistant.

However, wooing an assistant usually does not work if the assistant reports to someone at a high-level agency or for the head of a production company or a studio. Many of these assistants are what are known as "career" assistants who have no intention of becoming agents, producers, or studio execs.

There is a saying in Tinseltown that one should never scoff at an assistant. You just never know when he will end up being your boss!

The Business of Making Money

While most writers feel they should be generously rewarded for their submissions, the studios are obligated to make money for their stockholders. That responsibility means keeping an eagle's eye on production costs.

Did you know that the cost of the average theatrical motion picture without big name stars is approximately $50 million? That is for a film set in present day, with a minimum of stuntwork and special effects, no animals, and probably no children in any major roles. With the ever-rising cost of making movies, it makes sense for the savvy writer to consider what constitutes a "high-ticket" project.

Although knowing how to budget does not fall within the technical realm of screenplay writing, the high cost of moviemaking is a subject that affects anyone connected with the motion picture and television industries.

Let's look at some general areas that can send a movie's budget soaring:

Period Pieces/Futuristic Settings

This is an obvious high-ticket item in budgeting a theatrical or a television movie. A project set in the Middle Ages or Roaring '20s will require historically factual exterior and interior sets, props, modes of transportation, architecturally correct houses, and a time-specific wardrobe. Period pieces can also require additional research personnel.

While most major studios have sets for a Western street, a typical brownstone-lined New York avenue, or a Midwest main street, futuristic sets have to be assembled for each project. Stories set in the future carry the added cost of creating and making new props, backdrops, sets, furniture, vehicles, and costumes.

EXOTIC LOCATIONS

A spy thriller that takes place in five foreign cities also falls into the high-cost category. Although an audience loves to be swept away to an exotic land, the wise screenwriter sticks to one or two major locations. The exception, of course, is the **road story** in which characters are literally "on the road" from one location to the next as their story unfolds.

The role that time and budget constraints can play in challenging a writer is amazing. One popular film, *Three Days of the Condor*, was based on the book *Six Days of the Condor*, which involved several locations. In the interest of story clarity, timing, and budget, writer Lorenzo Semple Jr. needed to make sure his script addressed these issues. He ended up selecting the three most important days/incidents in the book, literally cutting the budget in half. The result was a highly entertaining and successful film which still maintained the book's original intent, suspense, and story integrity.

CHILDREN

While most child actors do not get millions of dollars per film, there are many strict guidelines and regulations you should be aware of that surround the filming of children. First, children are limited in the number of hours they may shoot per day. Thus, shooting with juveniles can take considerably more time. Overtime shooting is allowed only with a special permit and only if certain guidelines are met. And if there are night shots that require children, another permit is needed to accommodate night shooting.

The law also requires that an approved, paid tutor be hired for all children on the set under the age of eighteen, unless they are **emancipated minors** (have a high school equivalency or have obtained court permission to be on their own). In addition to a tutor, a classroom must be setup (whether at the studio or on location) and each child must receive a minimum of four hours of schooling per day. When minors are on the set, a child welfare supervisor must also be present.

Finally, we all need to remember that a child is a child. There can be a certain amount of unpredictability, depending on the child's age, disposition, and the shooting situation. For example, a young child told to run into a dark field on a chilly night may hesitate. The youngster may fear the dark, be too tired or cold, etc. Convincing a reluctant young actor who refuses to comply can be costly, especially if the writer ends up rewriting a scene.

But take heart: There are solutions. In some cases night scenes can be shot in daylight and merged with a night backdrop or shot with lighting that gives the appearance of night. The film *Adventures in Babysitting* could have been problematic, since most of the action takes place at night and the main characters portrayed are between six to eighteen years old. A number of special "blue screen" and "day for night" shots were used to give the illusion of night, thus keeping the costs down.

ANIMALS

As with children, there are strict guidelines regarding the use of animals on the set — from a herd of stampeding horses to animal stars like "Eddie," the dog on the popular television sitcom, *Frasier*. A paid SPCA supervisor must be present during all shots requiring animals. Any scenes where an animal is depicted as "injured" or "dead" must be carefully choreographed and approved by the SPCA supervisor before any filming can take place.

Scenes involving animals can take much longer to shoot. In addition to the supervision of camera coverage, the SPCA worker also carefully notes any cruelty, misconduct, or abuse in the handling, housing, and transporting of animals behind the scenes. There are limitations on the types of stunts animals can do and the length of time they can work in front of a camera each day. It is interesting, too, that some animals have "doubles" for more specific tasks like limping, climbing, etc.

STUNTWORK

Whenever there are fights, falls, chases, gunfights, fires, or any dangerous action, stunt doubles are required to take the place of most actors and actresses. And while it appears that nearly every movie or TV show seems to contain at least one car chase or fist fight, the stuntwork in those scenes does drive up the cost of the project. A car chase or a gun battle may take only a minute or two on the screen, but the actual time to set up, rehearse, and shoot the sequence from different angles may take days.

Also, stuntwork is highly dangerous, and stunt experts are well paid for their work. Unless you are intent on a big-budget action film, try to keep stuntwork uncomplicated and at a minimum.

High-Tech Special Effects

We have all seen films where fifty people are gunned down in a hail of Uzi fire while gas tankers explode all around them and the hero makes a getaway on some high-tech, super-charged, futuristic vehicle at warp speed into another time dimension… and that is only the opening sequence! But not every action film is a guaranteed box-office success. Satisfying what is viewed as the public's taste for mega-firepower no longer assures acceptance. High-tech effects alone will not sell your project, and the increased costs may actually do more harm than the effects do good.

The arena of high-tech special effects includes everything from fairly simple fade-outs to complex warp-speed chases in futuristic aircraft over the war fields of an unknown planet. Matte shots, blue screens, underwater sequences, explosions, disappearing or "morphing" objects, and any work requiring special cameras, models, miniatures, or recreated objects constitutes the ever-growing area of high-tech and special effects.

Also, to ensure that projects are technically accurate and appropriate, advisors or consultants are often hired to give their expert advice and opinions on everything from the complex NASA control center in *Apollo 13* to the realistic dinosaurs in the *Jurassic Park* series. For military dramas, armed-services experts are often hired to maintain the integrity of the weaponry and the personnel depicted on the screen.

The good news in this area is computers have greatly cut the costs on some special effects, allowing for slightly greater latitude.

A Cast of Thousands

Any project that requires hundreds of extras in crowd scenes carries an expensive price tag — think of having to provide wardrobe, props, makeup, and hairdressers for those crowds. The average extra makes about $100-$125 a day, not including the time need-ed for additional wardrobe or makeup calls. If you multiply this by 250 extras, that is $25,000-$30,000 for the extras alone, just to shoot one crowd scene.

Any extra asked to do something special (which can be anything from a close-up reaction to "fainting" to being the leader in a mob scene) will receive considerably more compensation per day. Plus, all union extras receive benefits paid by the production com-pany through the union, driving up the price of those crowd scenes even more.

BALANCING ACT

The above big-ticket items are not meant to deter writers from creating memorable movies. They are meant as additional infor-mation in helping you to balance your plot and shape your proj-ect to make it even more desirable in the eyes of potential buyers. If your project contains more than three or four of these high-cost items, you may want to take a second look to see if there is any way to keep the expenses down.

WHAT IS THE WGA?

Throughout this book, you will see the initials WGA. They stand for the Writers Guild of America. Members that live east of the Mississippi belong to WGA, East (aka WGAe). If members live west of the Mississippi, they belong to WGA, West (aka WGAw).

The WGA is the union which represents writers primarily for the purpose of collective bargaining in the motion picture, television, and radio industries. The WGA has recently stepped in to represent writers of new media and animation as well.

New screenwriters who have yet to join the Guild often falsely assume that obtaining membership means instant and constant employment. While most major studios and larger production companies are signatories to the WGA and employ screenwriters who usually belong to the Guild, the number of writers far exceeds the number of assignments available. The WGA does not obtain writing assignments, offer writing instruction, or accept material for submission to production companies.

WHY IS THE WGA SO IMPORTANT?

Once a screenwriter has obtained enough "units of credit" (currently twenty-four units within three years of application), he will likely join the WGA for the following reasons:

- Non-union writers usually make considerably less than WGA members.

- Non-union writers usually are not covered by the WGA's health and pension plans.

- Non-union writers usually find it a costly venture for them when disputes occur involving writing credits.

HOW CAN THE SERVICES OF THE WGA BENEFIT A NON-MEMBER?

Besides providing its members with basic minimum wage guidelines and working conditions, excellent benefits, and recognized authority in determining writing credits, the Guild also provides the following services (many of these services are made available to non-members as a courtesy for a small fee):

• The Television Market List features contact-submission information on current weekly primetime television programs. This list is published monthly in the WGAw *Written By*, which non-members can also obtain for a nominal subscription fee. *Written By* also contains articles on industry issues, interviews with WGA members, and provides an FYI page listing helpful numbers for researching in Southern California.

• The WGA Signatory Agency Listing features literary agencies that are affiliated with the WGA. This listing is updated several times a year and contains agencies that are currently open to submissions or queries from new writers. If you are not certain that an agent or an agency you are dealing with is a WGA signatory, you can call the Guild and ask for the Agency Verification Department. If an "agent" asks for fees up front or violates any of the WGA guidelines, you can contact the WGA to file a complaint.

• The Professional Writer's Teleplay/Screenplay Format Guide features helpful information on the industry-accepted script format and is available to both members and non-members.

• The WGA Registration Service provides assistance to both members and non-members in establishing the completion date and the identity of their literary properties written for the entertainment industry. While this registration does not give a writer statutory protection, it does provide a record of a writer's claim to authorship of the material involved and of the date of its completion. Placing the words "Registered with the WGA" on the bottom corner of the title page of your script also is a subtle warning against possible plagiarism. Registration is currently $20 for non-members per project (i.e., outline, synopsis, teleplay, treatment, or screenplay).

• The Minimum Basic Agreement provides the guidelines for employment, working conditions, and minimum basic wages for its members who work with signatory studios and production entities. Knowing what these minimum wages are can be especially useful if an emerging writer is lucky enough to have a producer or a studio express interest in purchasing his work.

• The Directory of WGA Members lists current WGA members and their produced credits. Producers and execs often use this directory when looking for a writer for an in-house idea, a polish, or a rewrite. This directory is also handy for writers who want to look up the author of their favorite movie.

HOW CAN I OBTAIN MORE INFORMATION?

For more detailed information on the WGA and the services it offers, you can reach the Guild at:

WGA West
7000 West Third St.
Los Angeles CA 90048
(323)951-4000
www.wga.org

WGA East
555 West 57th St. #1230
New York, NY 10019
(212)767-7800
www.wgaeast.org

PART II – MEETINGS AND PITCHES

CHAPTER 3

PITCHING — A NECESSARY EVIL

True story from a writer who wishes to remain anonymous: When he was getting started in the business and wanted to make an impression on a high-powered producer, the writer came in to "pitch" his baseball movie, dressed in a baseball uniform, complete with ball and mitt. To start out his pitch, he tossed the ball to the producer to get his attention and to emphasize that the name of the project was *The Catch*. Unfortunately, the writer's aim was off and the ball hit the producer's coffee mug, spilling java all over the place. The writer admitted he needed lessons in how to pitch.

Pitching is the art of communicating (verbally or in writing) the essence of your screenplay or project, usually to an agent, a studio executive, or a producer. While fewer projects are optioned on a pitch alone, more writers are pitching their wares as a means of enticing potential buyers to read their completed scripts.

Pitchfests, weekend marathons of pitching to potential buyers, are also major components of many screenwriting conferences. **One-on-Ones**, ten-minute meetings with featured speakers or presenters, are also guaranteed "draws" for writers to attend and have the opportunity to tell Hollywood execs about their latest and greatest projects.

Pitching, especially the verbal kind, does not come naturally to most writers. After all, writers seem to prefer to let their words-on-paper do most of the talking for them. With the high volume of never-ending scripts flooding the studios and the major production companies every month, pitching has become "a necessary evil" for screenwriters to face and conquer.

Did you know that there are different types of pitches? And do you know when to utilize them to "sell" your work? Let's go over the types of pitches you are most likely to use.

Elevator Pitch

You are attending a film festival. You get into the elevator of a posh hotel and notice there is only one other person in the elevator with you. It is Clint Eastwood, who just happens to be the perfect actor for the lead role in your very latest screenplay. He presses the tenth floor button. You recognize that this may be your golden opportunity and you have approximately ten to fifteen seconds to tell him about your project.

While this scenario may seem highly unlikely, having less than a minute to tell someone about your project *is* a very common situation. Would you be able to tell your story in less than a minute? For many writers, this is sheer terror. But, with preparation, the "elevator pitch" can be one of your most useful selling tools. Here's an elevator pitch which might have enticed Clint Eastwood into starring in *In the Line of Fire*:

EXAMPLE:
An aging Secret Service agent goes after a deranged would-be assassin who plays mind games by reminding the agent of his one big failure: The agent was unable to prevent the assassination of President John F. Kennedy. As he's tracking the assassin, the agent must also prove himself in the eyes of his rookie partner and the rest of the presidential Secret Service squad, including an attractive female agent.

An elevator pitch should not take more than ten to thirty seconds and should be no more than a few sentences in length. The first sentence clearly lays out the major storyline and even brings in the main character's motivating backstory, which will propel him throughout most of the movie. The second sentence also provides the groundwork for the sub-story: the romance between Clint Eastwood's character and the attractive female agent. The overall pitch signals an intriguing plot that combines danger, action, suspense, and romance with a complex lead character who is facing a nefarious foe.

The elevator pitch is what many writers use at the fast-paced pitchfests where the producers and the development execs only want to hear a couple of sentences about your project before deciding if they want to hear more details. The elevator pitch is a slightly longer **logline** (a one- or two- sentence summation of a movie), which can serve as a setup for your five-minute pitch.

A written version of the elevator pitch can also be used as a major component of a writer's query letter to producers or agents, which brings us to the next type of pitch.

THE PITCH ON PAPER

Many a well-prepared writer has given thanks to those fickle screenwriting Muses for having a **P.O.P.** or pitch on paper. A pitch on paper is your movie laid out in written form. It is a brief, one-page synopsis of your project, which has just enough details to whet a producer's or agent's appetite and to distinguish your project from others.

Basically, the P.O.P. consists of the following:

- A logline that gives the potential buyer a general idea of the storyline

- The first paragraph that contains the setup of the story — the main character, his present situation, his enemy/foe, where the story takes place, and the character(s) and incident that moves the main character into action

- The second paragraph that is a brief overview of the challenges the hero or the heroine must face in the mid-section of the movie

- The third paragraph that is a quick summation of the ending or a summation of Act III that ends with an intriguing question or situation designed to leave the climax to the imagination of the potential buyer

Here is how *Sleepless In Seattle* may have looked as a pitch on paper:

EXAMPLE:

LOGLINE: A young boy's call to a radio psychologist sets into motion a series of events which could unite his widowed father with a magazine writer. Only a couple of things stand in the way: The boy and his father live in Seattle, and the writer is already engaged and lives in Baltimore.

SAM is a Seattle architect, a widower, and father to young JONAH. Jonah recognizes his father is lonely. Troubled, Jonah calls one of those late-night radio psychologists and talks about how worried he is for his dad. In Baltimore, a magazine writer, ANNIE, and her FIANCE have just announced their engagement to her family. As she's driving home, she tunes into the talk show and feels a connection to Sam. Annie's best friend BECKY suggests that she do an article on radio talk shows. Realizing that Jonah is right and he needs to get on with his life, Sam contemplates dating again.

Sam takes the plunge and calls the DECORATOR on one of his projects. She ends up asking him for a date. Annie writes a letter to "Sleepless in Seattle," the radio psychologist's nickname for Sam, but tosses it in the trash. Becky rescues the letter and sends it off to Seattle. Unable to get "Sleepless in Seattle" out of her mind, Annie arrives in Seattle to do her story. She sees Sam embracing another woman and quickly returns home.

Annie plunges back into her wedding planning with her Fiancé, while Sam makes plans to spend the weekend with the Decorator, much to the disappointment of Jonah, who sneaks out of the house and takes a flight to NYC, hoping to meet Annie at the top of the Empire State Building. Will Sam realize where Jonah has gone? Will Annie listen to her heart? And will Sam and Annie finally meet?

Note that most of the storyline is set up in the first paragraph and fewer details are given in the second and third paragraphs. In summation, each of the paragraphs coincides with the basic three-act structure: beginning, middle, and end.

Some writers prefer to do one long paragraph for their pitch on paper, which is basically two sentences on each act. A P.O.P. is sometimes given to a potential buyer at the end of a pitch meeting — to help the producer or the exec refresh her memory after a day of hearing several pitches. Some agents or smaller production companies might be intrigued by your query letter, but are not yet willing to take the time to commit to looking at a 110-page script. They may ask you for a one-page synopsis (or P.O.P.) of your project.

THE BIG PITCH
For those situations when you have a one-on-one consultation or a potential buyer is intrigued by your logline or elevator pitch and wants to hear more, you should be ready for the "Big Pitch."

Writers should approach the Big Pitch as a "verbal trailer" for the film they envision. Like the visual trailer or coming attraction, this pitch should contain the highlights of the story you are telling and should be told with confidence and style.

A concise, well-told story can either open or close career doors for a writer. Here are some pointers if you are fortunate enough to be invited to pitch your project at a studio or a production company:

BE CONCISE
Know in advance that most pitch meetings will last less than 20–30 minutes, tops. Most of the meeting will consist of general

introductory small talk before the pitch. In most cases, the actual pitch will take anywhere from five to seven minutes, although five minutes is probably preferable. After the pitch, time is allowed for any questions or suggestions from the potential buyer, followed by some parting inquiries or comments from you, the writer.

KNOW YOUR AUDIENCE

Research the studio or the production company where you will be pitching. What kinds of movies or television projects do they produce? More importantly, what kinds of projects do they *not* produce?

For example, a writer once made the mistake of pitching a slasher movie to the execs at Walt Disney Pictures. Needless to say, it was an immediate "pass" and left the executives with the impression that the writer had not spent much time researching the studio's development slate.

There is no excuse for not researching a studio or a production company in advance of a meeting. The *Hollywood Creative Directory's Producers* lists credits for produced work beneath each production entity's name. And many production companies now have Web sites listing their produced credits. The key is to look for studios and production companies who have shown an interest in producing films in the same genre as your own.

In addition, it is important to keep up to date on any "deals" that a studio or production company may have made recently, especially with actors or directors who may have a production company on the premises. Reading the **trade papers** (*The Hollywood Reporter*, *Variety*) can often yield this type of valuable information. Again, the *Hollywood Creative Directory's Producers* has a section in the back which cross-references personnel with the names of production companies and studios with whom they are connected.

PRACTICE MAKES PERFECT

It's common sense: Practice your pitch beforehand. It is best to practice in front of people who are *not* familiar with your story. This rehersal will help to focus on any sticky plot points or confusing story lines.

While practicing in front of your parents, spouse, or siblings can provide some comfort and reassurance, you will get a much more honest appraisal of your work if you pitch your project in front of your writers group or a friend who works in marketing or sales.

Be sure to ask the following questions after practicing your pitch in front of your group or friends:

- Did they have any comments or suggestions?

- Did they get a feel for the characters?

- Did they understand what the hero/heroine was trying to accomplish?

- Did any sections of the pitch feel too slow or too fast?

- Was the storyline logical and clearly laid out or were there any confusing pieces of plotting?

- Is this a movie that they would pay to see?

- If not, why?

HAVE A BACKUP

Be ready to pitch two projects, knowing that you will probably only have time to pitch one. This preparation is especially handy when you have invested time and money in attending a pitchfest.

Why have a backup pitch? If the executive or agent you are pitching to does not appear attentive when you are halfway through, you can quickly wind up your story and go on to your next project.

Also, you never know when a potential buyer will ask if you have other projects in the works. A true writer always has several projects in the works.

SHOW SOME STYLE

Be enthusiastic when you pitch. Keep in mind that studio and production execs listen to as many as five to six pitches every day. Having heard hundreds of pitches, I can assure you there is nothing worse than someone who is mumbling his story into his lap.

You can ham it up a bit, but do not let your theatrics overshadow your story. Here's an instance where someone went "over the top":

The project was a modern-day version of the popular fairy tale *Cinderella*. Every time the Fairy Godmother was mentioned in the pitch, the writer threw "magic dust" into the air and waved a "magic wand." By the end of the pitch, my hair and my office were covered with gold and silver glitter. I remembered the pitch — but not for the right reasons!

Here's a case where someone used just the right amount of theatrics:

To emphasize her 1960s nostalgic setting, a writer started out by playing the first sixteen bars of a popular song from that era before launching into her pitch. She's not sure if the musical introduction was responsible, but it got the executive to listen attentively to her pitch... which was optioned on the spot!

Remember to speak clearly — not too quickly and not too slowly. Look at the buyer when you are pitching. It is fine to refer to your notes from time to time, but do not "read" your movie.

START WITH A LOGLINE

Start off with your logline, which should accurately convey the essence of your movie as well as a sense of why the public should rush to see it Think of the **one-sheets** (giant posters) that advertise the movie (and see page 82).

Some writers often use other successful projects to convey a sense of story and tone.

EXAMPLE:

A Puerto Rican barrio in New York serves as the backdrop for a star-crossed romance à la *Romeo and Juliet*. (*West Side Story*)

GO ON TO THE BASICS

Next, state the genre, time period, and where a majority of the action takes place.

EXAMPLE:
This contemporary bi-coastal romantic-comedy takes place in Seattle and Baltimore. (*Sleepless in Seattle*)

It is important to state the genre at the beginning of the pitch as a means of setting the scene and the tone of the project. I once had a meeting with a writer who obviously hated pitching and did not show much inflection or emotion in his pitch. Thus, I thought the project was a drama and informed him that we'd recently bought a number of dramatic projects. We both were embarrassed when he declared that his project was, in fact, a comedy!

INTRODUCE YOUR MAIN CHARACTERS
Introduce your main characters with a brief but "telling" description which gives such information as age range, major personality traits, job/career, etc.

EXAMPLE:
Axel Foley, 20s, is a get-it-done Detroit cop who never quite follows the book. (*Beverly Hills Cop*)

And while there is no need to introduce every single character in your screenplay, do not forget to include the antagonist and any secondary characters who have a major impact on the storyline.

HIT THE HIGH NOTES
Stick to the major plot points and character revelations only. There is no need to describe each and every scene, but any subplot that is key to the main storyline should also be mentioned to give an idea of the depth of the story.

It is also helpful to indicate where you are from time to time.

EXAMPLE:
By the end of Act I, Axel is thrown out of Maitland's Beverly Hills office building — Axel is ready to declare war. (*Beverly Hills Cop*)

This technique lets the executive or the producer know you are aware of key plot points and story structure.

ALLOW FOR DISCUSSION

Afterwards, allow a few minutes for any questions and comments from the executive or the producer. You may be asked and should be prepared to answer the following:

- Do you have a completed script or treatment on this project? (Most potential buyers will not schedule a pitch meeting unless you do.)

- Does your project have any **attachments** (that is, a committed producer, actor, or director)? Do not worry if you do not have attachments, as many venues prefer projects with as few encumbrances as possible.

Some buyers play it close to the vest and may not have any comments other than "We'll get back to you." On occasion, some will pass on the spot.

However, if a producer/executive liked your previous work and if your pitch was well told, you may be asked to contact the producer when your next screenplay is close to completion, even if the project you just pitched does not fit into her present development plans.

This is also the perfect time to ask what is on the studio or production company's "wish list" of projects. What genre of films are they looking for? If you have a project that might be suitable, it is appropriate to mention it. If the potential buyer has the time, he may even ask you to tell him a little bit about it. But if he does not ask you about the project, do not force the issue.

BE RECEPTIVE

In general, be open to all comments and responses given. You might file suggestions in a feedback file.

More specifically, if the same plot point is questioned by different potential buyers, consider reworking and clarifying that particular area of the project.

Do not be surprised if an executive or a producer tells you she (or another studio/company) has something similar in development. Similar story ideas seem to come in waves (remember *18 Again*, *Vice-Versa*, and *Big*?). Few people remember the first two films mentioned, but most people fondly recall *Big*, which was released last but was the most successful of the three movies in which the protagonist changed ages, either starting as an adult and becoming a child or vice-versa. "Something similar" does not mean someone's "stolen" your idea. "Something similar" can mean a project is set in the same historical period or has a very similar "hook" as your idea.

BE PREPARED

If the buyer shows an interest in your pitch, ask if she would like to see the screenplay. If you have not completed your screenplay, give her an idea of when it might be completed.

Legally, the buyer cannot ask a writer for written material without his agent's or entertainment attorney's knowledge, but many writers carry a P.O.P. and hand it out at the end of the meeting. Just be sure your name, your agent's name (if you have one), address, e-mail, and phone information are also included.

Since executives and producers hear dozens of pitches each week, they may need a summary to refer to if they want to take further action on your project. Most writers would rather have a potential buyer refer to a summary they have written than to rely on the exec's or producer's memory.

If a buyer is "high" on your pitch and asks to see the script, have a copy available. If you do not have an agent, request a release form (see page 190). If you have an agent, call the agent immediately after the meeting and let her know that a script of your project is with John X at Z Films, so she can record the information and follow up on it.

Do Not Give Up
Keep in mind that there are more than one studio or production company around. One rejection does not indicate failure.

If, however, you have pitched your project to several entities without so much as a nibble, you may want to consider shifting the focus of your efforts on your next project and put the first one aside.

Distance and time will sometimes yield new ideas and insights that can improve your initial work.

Remember that a pitch meeting is usually only given to writers whose work has been favorably read. If you are fortunate enough to have obtained a pitch meeting, make sure you are well prepared. Because time is at a premium, writers (especially those who are less experienced or "unproduced") may not get another opportunity to pitch to the same person again, unless that initial pitch is exceptionally well told.

CHAPTER 4

TALKIN' THE TALK — INDUSTRY-SPEAK AKA WHAT THE HELL ARE THEY TALKING ABOUT?

One of my clients from Canada had his first meeting with a production company. I called and asked him how the meeting went. He excitedly told me how the producer and his development director were both dressed in black, and talked about "*attaching*" something to his script, how the story could be "*franchised*," and that they needed to know who was "*fronting*" him and whether there would be enough room for a "*back end*."

He then paused to ask, "So is this good or bad?"

While you are attending a writers conference, a pitchfest, or a film festival, or perusing the trade papers or anticipating your first Hollywood meeting, you will likely become aware that there are a number of strange-sounding phrases and terms being bantered about. These "buzz words" are peppered throughout the conversations of industry-related personnel. You know they're speaking English, but *what kind*? You are probably overhearing what is commonly called *industry-speak*. No, it is not exactly a foreign language, but it is a language of terms that are common to people who are involved in the day-to-day running of the entertainment industry.

In order to help you fully understand what is going on in Hollywood, as well as keep you one step ahead of many other emerging writers, it is wise to have a working knowledge of some of these phrases and terms. To better acquaint you with them and what they really mean, let's follow a fictitious new screenwriting duo (we will call them Lauren and Joel), who are about to experience their first brush with success in Hollywood — let's keep in mind that this could be *YOU*!

ONCE UPON A TIME – THE PRESENT

JOEL and LAUREN are attending a writers conference for their very first time. They are almost finished with their script, an exciting adventure project. They feel the timing is right to give Hollywood a try. Because they registered early at the conference, they are given a coveted ten-minute appointment with a well-known PRODUCER.

The Producer asks, "So what's the *logline* on your *spec* and is it *high concept* or *low concept*? Is it a theatrical film or is it more appropriate as a *MOW*?"

WHAT HE REALLY MEANS: "Give me an exciting one- or two-sentence summary (**logline**) on your script (written on **speculation**, i.e., without pay) and tell me if it's commercial enough for mass audience appeal (**high concept**) or is it a more specialized, narrowly-focused movie that will have a more limited audience appeal (**low concept**)?" The Producer also wants to know if the project being pitched is a traditional theatrical motion picture or a Movie of the Week (**MOW**) meant for television or cable.

Joel and Lauren are prepared with their logline and proceed to pitch their story. The Producer asks for clarification on the hero's *character arc*. Lauren and Joel quickly explain how the main character transforms himself from an ordinary Joe into a courageous and resourceful hero who learns that victory is not about strength of body, but strength of inner resolve. Now the Producer is clearly showing some interest and queries: "So who's getting *story by* and who's getting *written by* credits?"

WHAT HE REALLY MEANS: "What is the main character trying to achieve, not only physically, but emotionally or spiritually (**character arc**)?" and "Did both of you come up with the story and are both of you writing the screenplay, or did one of you come up with the story and the other is going to write the script?" The Producer is trying to establish each person's actual participation in this project. **Story by** simply means who came up with the basic storyline and the main characters for the script. **Written by** simply means who is writing the actual script that is based on that story. In addition to clarifying their credits on the screen, each person's participation can often determine the actual division of monies, should a project be sold.

After establishing that Joel came up with the storyline and both Joel and Lauren will be writing the script, the Producer asks: "Are there any *attachments*? Are you registered with *the Guild*?"

WHAT HE'S REALLY ASKING: Is there a director or actor/actress who has agreed to be in this project (**attachment**) if it is set-up with a distributor and/or financing is acquired? The Producer also wants to know if Lauren and Joel have registered their material with the **Writers Guild of America**, which serves as the union representing screenwriters.

Lauren tells the Producer that there are no attachments to their project, which is registered with the WGA. Lauren would also like the opportunity to direct, to which the Producer comments, "So you're looking to become a *hyphenate*?"

WHAT HE REALLY MEANS: "So you're interested in becoming a writer-director?" A **hyphenate** is a person who receives more than one credit on the same project, such as a writer-producer or a writer-director. George Lucas of *Star Wars* fame is a hyphenate, as is Mel Gibson who served as actor-producer-director for the Oscar-winning film *Braveheart*.

Joel quickly chimes in that he is confident their project has the potential to be turned into a television series if the movie is a success. The Producer, sensing a possible *franchise*, responds, "Have you already written a *pilot* and a *bible*?"

WHAT HE'S REALLY ASKING: "Have you written the first introductory episode (**pilot**) as well as a detailed personality breakdown of the characters, how they relate to one another, the setup of the series, and what ties the episodes together (**bible**)? A **franchise** is when a project can be spun-off and have more than one application (i.e., television series, video games, amusement park attraction/ride, sequel, etc.).

Unfortunately, Lauren and Joel have not written a pilot or a bible for a television series based on their project. The producer expresses his interest in the project as a film, but rather than wait for another month for them to finish writing the screenplay, he asks, "Have you written a *treatment* yet?"

WHAT HE'S REALLY ASKING FOR: A **treatment** is generally a five-to ten-page document which will give the Producer all the major plot points and important details of the script, as well as an indication of the project's general structure and character interactions.

Joel and Lauren just happen to have a treatment with them and hand it to the Producer after first asking for, then signing a *release form.*

WHAT THEY ASKED FOR: To avoid any possible legal problems, Joel and Lauren know that they need to have a written record that the Producer has seen their treatment. Signing a **release form** protects both the writers and the Producer.

A FEW DAYS LATER
The Producer has read the treatment and loves it! He is interested in seeing the script when it is done. Joel and Lauren are having second thoughts and want to submit the material to all the major studios on their own. The Producer tells them, "None of the studios will accept an *unsolicited* piece of work."

WHAT HE REALLY MEANS: The studios have strict legal policies which prevent them from accepting material from anyone unless the material is submitted by a producer, an agent, or an entertainment attorney. Material that comes to a studio, an agency, or a production company without representation is considered **unsolicited.** He wants them to understand that if they stick with him, they will have a better chance of having their work accepted.

He asks, "Do you two have a *Guild-signatory ten-percenter?*"

WHAT HE'S REALLY ASKING: "Are Lauren and Joel represented by an agent who is affiliated and approved (a **signatory**) by the Writers Guild of America?" The term **ten-percenter** refers to the ten-percent commission that agents make when they sell a writer's work.

Joel and Lauren tell the Producer they do not have an agent yet, but would love to have a referral from the Producer. Eager to maintain his interest in Joel and Lauren's project, he tells them he would be happy to place a call to an AGENT he has done business with at a small but respected agency. He tells the Agent that he is interested in the adventure project that the writers are working on, but they do not have representation. Would the Agent be willing to look at their script and consider *fronting* them on this project?

WHAT HE'S REALLY ASKING: Would the Agent do him a favor and look at Joel and Lauren's screenplay and consider representing (**fronting**) them on this project?

Three Weeks Later

Joel and Lauren have finished their script and the Producer has given it to the Agent, who agrees to represent them. The Agent thinks, "The project would be better if it were *packaged.*"

WHAT HE REALLY MEANS: The Agent feels the project could be more desirable to a potential studio if he added a **name** (well-known) director or actor/actress who could bring the project more prestige or appeal. **Packaging** is the process of putting the talent (and often the financing) together with the script.

The Producer tells the Agent he will take his chances without packaging the project, but he needs to take the project to Studio A first because he has a *housekeeping deal* with them.

WHAT HE REALLY MEANS: He has an arrangement with Studio A. They provide him with an office and a small staff (**housekeeping deal**). In exchange he is required to bring all of his projects to Studio A first before taking them anywhere else. This is also referred to as a **first-look deal**.

Joel and Lauren's script is sent to Studio A's Story Department for *coverage* where the story analyst will read and evaluate the project. Nine out of ten of the scripts that cross the reader's desk are a *Pasadena*.

WHAT THIS REALLY MEANS: The story analyst will write up a report (**coverage**) that consists of a logline, a detailed synopsis, and a commentary that is based on such factors as characterization, dialogue, budgeting, pacing, originality of story idea, structure, etc. If the analyst rejects or passes on a project, it is often referred to in unflattering terms as a **Pasadena**.

In this case, Joel and Lauren's script is given very good marks and is shown to the rest of the *creative group*. The Producer knows that unless Act I immediately captures the executives' interest, some of them may resort to the dreaded *30/10* read.

WHAT THIS REALLY MEANS: Joel and Lauren's screenplay is to be read by the directors of development (or creative execs) and the vice presidents and senior/executive vice presidents of production (**creative group**) to see if they agree with the analyst's assessment that this project has the potential to be considered for their production development line-up. The Producer knows that if the script does not "hook" the executives in the first 20–30 pages, the execs will be sorely tempted to simply skip to the concluding ten pages just to see how the story ends, leaving a vast majority of the script unread (**30/10 read**).

Studio A asks if the Producer has *optioned* the project or if it was an outright *sale*.

WHAT THIS REALLY MEANS: Studio A is merely trying to determine if the Producer put up a fee entitling him to "temporary" exclusive rights to the project for a mutually agreeable period of time (**option**) or if the Producer bought the script "outright" (**sale**). The Studio wants to know what the legal status of the project is, so they can factor in how much money they will need to reimburse the Producer before they become involved in a deal which will ultimately bring them sole ownership rights to the project.

Studio A is not sure it wants to do such a high-budgeted project. The Agent steps in and tells Studio A that Studio B has heard about the project and is eager to do business with the Producer. Studio A feels the *heat* and realizes a *bidding war* may ensue, so its execs decide to make a quick, lucrative deal.

WHAT THIS REALLY MEANS: When Studio A's interest seemed to waver, the Agent (as a courtesy) let them know of another studio's interest. This put pressure, intense interest, and focused hype (**heat**) on the project. Studio A did not want to get into a situation where it would be in an escalating financial high-stakes competition (**bidding war**) for Lauren and Joel's project.

The Studio makes a deal with the Producer and gives Joel and Lauren *$200,000 against $400,000*. The Studio gives the Producer his usual fee plus *points*. The project is then assigned to a creative team of executives who will *shepherd* the script through *development*. The Producer tells Joel and Lauren that he hopes they will not have to go through *development hell*.

WHAT THIS REALLY MEANS: Joel and Lauren will receive $200,000 for the sale of their script. If the project is produced, they will receive additional monies for a total deal of $400,000 (**$200,000 against $400,000**). In addition to his usual producer's fee, the Producer — who has produced several successful movies — is given certain percentage **points** if the movie makes a profit. The creative team of a senior/executive vice president and a director of development will guide the project (**shepherd**) as they work with the Producer and the writers to hopefully improve and hone a script through each revision (**development**). Occasionally, egos, budgets, and other hard-to-control variables intrude upon the process, making the working relationship very volatile and turning the situation into a negative one (**development hell**).

The first set of *development notes* mentions such comments as *Morse Code* and *on-the-nose*, and the *lead shepherd* wonders if the next revision will have to be a *page-oner*.

WHAT'S ACTUALLY BEING SAID: The first detailed memo of suggestions (**development notes**) written by the creative team addresses the project's storytelling weakness of giving away too much of the plot in advance (**Morse Code, aka telegraphing the plot**). The notes also mention that the writers have a tendency to write dialogue that explains things in a very obvious manner and is, therefore, too **on-the-nose**. The senior or executive vice president of the creative team (**lead shepherd**) is not sure if the writers will have to do a complete revision, starting from the very beginning (**page-oner**).

After a series of revisions the creative group thinks the project is in good enough shape to attach a director or a star so the project can be *greenlighted*. Director X and Actress Z are interested and will have a *pay-or-play* deal with significant *back-end participation*.

WHAT'S REALLY BEING SAID: The script is ready to put a director and actor/actress on the project so it can be approved for filming (**greenlighted**). The agents or attorneys for Director X and Actress Z want their clients to have a provision in their contracts that states they will each be paid their full salaries even if the movie is never made (**pay-or-play**). This is a form of insurance policy for the director and actor/actress since much sought-after talent would not be available for other possible offers if they are committed to work on this project. This clause is only given to talent with a history of successful films under their belts. Also, some top-name stars and directors will often negotiate a clause which gives them a percentage of the profits after a film has been released (**back-end participation**).

Studio A tells Joel, Lauren, and the Producer that Actress Z brings a lot of *star baggage* to the project which could spell trouble. But the deal is struck and the project is about to go into *preproduction* when the head of production is given an *indie prod deal* and the new head of production puts the project into *turnaround*.

WHAT THIS REALLY MEANS: Actress Z wants to throw a lot of added expenses into her contract, such as specially designed dressing rooms, high-priced hair stylists, make-up artists, fitness trainers, therapists, etc. (**star baggage**). When a project is given the "go-ahead" to cast all the characters, find locations, hire a crew, design sets, costumes, and props, etc., this process is known as **preproduction**. It takes place from the time the script is given the **greenlight** until the time actual filming begins. When the head of production is fired, a studio sometimes pays off the rest of his contract by giving him an independent production deal (**indie prod deal**), which means he can buy and develop films as a producer with a first-look deal on the studio lot. For one reason or another, the new head of production may decide not to go ahead with Joel and Lauren's project and will put it on inactive status (**turnaround**), in hopes that Studio B or any competitors may want to pay all the costs incurred to buy the project.

As luck would have it, the Agent has contacted Studio B, who is interested in Joel and Lauren's project. Studio B suggests that they will pay half the costs to Studio A and go into a *co-production* or *joint venture*. Studio A readily agrees to this. Joel and Lauren's movie makes it to the big screen and is considered *boffo*.

THE HAPPY ENDING
Realizing that sharing the costs is much less of a risk, Studio A and Studio B go into partnership together on agreed-upon costs (**co-production** or **joint venture**). Joel and Lauren's script becomes a film with great box office success (**boffo**).

Please note that many of the above terms are explained in depth in Chapter 7.

CHAPTER 5

TAKING A MEETING — WHAT TO DO WHEN YOU MEET THE MOGULS

A writer was excited about his first meeting with a bigwig at one of the networks. Unfortunately, his appointment was on September 11, 2001, so his meeting had to be re-scheduled. Realizing his project (a one-hour drama series about a crack team of government agents on special assignment) might not be appropriate in light of recent events, the writer changed his drama into an ensemble comedy, which actually interested the exec. Although he turned the series down, the bigwig got the writer another meeting with an important **show-runner** (producer with a proven track record of television series), who hired the writer as a story editor on one of his hit shows.

INT. — YOUR LIVINGROOM — DAY
The phone RINGS.   YOU answer the phone.

>   YOUR AGENT
>   Guess what? Spielberg just
>   read your latest screenplay.
>   He wants to meet with you next
>   week.

You collapse to the floor, visibly shaken.

>   YOUR AGENT
>   Are you still there?
>   Do you wanna take the
>   meeting or not?

You pick yourself off the floor.

>   YOU
>   (being nobody's fool)
>   Yes… of course!!!!

CUT TO

EXT./INT. — AMBLIN ENTERTAINMENT - DAY

You confidently stride from the parking lot into
Spielberg's terra-cotta, adobe-walled, Santa-Fe-
style bungalow, carrying under your arm the
screenplay that you just know will be his latest
and ultimately best film ever. A cocky smile
crosses your face as you enter.

EXT. — AMBLIN ENTERTAINMENT — LATER

```
SPIELBERG shakes your hand as you are leaving
Amblin.  You strut away with a multimillion-dollar
check in your pocket.  As Spielberg closes the
door, you give a fist pump worthy of Tiger Woods.

FADE OUT
```

While the scenario above is every scriptwriter's dream, hearing the words "We'd like to meet with you" can send tremors of fear into the hearts of many a writer, novice and veteran alike. Such was the case with an emerging writer I knew. She received a call from an assistant, asking if she could meet with a big-time producer. While she hastily agreed to the meeting, she realized, after hanging up the phone, that she did not have a clue about what was expected of her at this, her very first "Hollywood" meeting.

If you are fortunate enough to receive a call from a Hollywood professional asking if you would like to "take a meeting," knowing what is ahead can help you prepare — both mentally and emotionally.

Here are some suggestions for what to do when you get your big opportunity to "meet and greet Hollywood":

GATHER SOME BACKGROUND
First, if you have an agent or a manager, ask him to find out how the meeting came about.

- Did a producer or an executive read some of your work? If so, which script(s) were read?

- Is the producer taking this meeting at the request of your agent?

- Did the caller specify whether the company is interested in purchasing this screenplay, or is this a request for a "get-acquainted" meeting based on the fact that someone liked your work?

- Is the producer open to hearing new ideas at this meeting?

- If so, does the agent know what is on her wish list?

If you do not have an agent, you should still try to track down the source of the request, if possible.

- Did you send a recent script or query letter to this producer or exec?

- Did you just win a screenwriting competition or make the finals in a script contest?

- Was this a speaker or a presenter you met at a writing conference or an industry-networking event who may have liked your pitch?

In most cases, the producer or the executive requesting the meeting has probably read at least one of your screenplays or heard about your latest script and obviously feels you possess talent. But be forewarned: The meeting may not necessarily signal a sale or an option for you. In fact, unless your agent or the person calling you specifically mentions significant interest in your script, chances are a sale or an option will not be in the offering.

In all likelihood, the producer or the exec may want to find out what other material you have written or are in the process of writing.

Perhaps the company or the studio has an open writing assignment — either to rewrite an existing project or to write an in-house idea — and your recent submission may be in the same genre or category.

Before the meeting, it would be wise to do some research of your own. Some of the basic information you should gather beforehand includes the following:

- What are the company's most recent credits (both successes and failures)?

- With whom will you be meeting? What is his title? What are his responsibilities?

- Does the company prefer high- or soft-concept projects, or does it seem to produce a mixture of both?

- Does the company produce low-, medium-, or high-budget films or films with a wide range of budgets?

- Does the company seem to concentrate on certain movie genres (e.g., dramas, comedies, thrillers, etc.)?

- Do the films seem geared for a specific audience (e.g., children, families, young adult males, women, etc.)?

- Who were the major players in the company's last few productions (e.g., actors, actresses, directors, etc.)?

If the company is a television production house or cable or network entity, you should find out the following information:

- Does the company produce mostly TV series, Movies of the Week, mini-series, or specials?

- Is the emphasis on comedies, dramas, animation, or children's programming?

- Do any actors/actresses have "deals" with the company?

Why does a writer need to know all of this? Here are just a couple of very good reasons for being forearmed:

- You can use much of the information as an ice breaker. All producers and executives enjoy talking about their projects; such a conversation is an excellent way to let them know that you are not only knowledgeable about the industry, but also specifically interested in their production company/studio.

- You can also use what you have learned to help select a couple of appropriate projects (either written or partially written) that might be suitable for their company. That way, if you are asked what you are working on, you will be prepared with a project that is more likely to fit into their general development slate. It is not a bad idea to work on a five- to seven-minute pitch, just in case.

PLAN THE LOGISTICS
If you are coming to the meeting from a considerable distance, you may want to arrive the day before, if possible. Then you will

have adequate time to check into the hotel, rest (especially if you are coming from another time zone), and get clear-cut instructions on how to go to the studio or production company.

If you are driving to the meeting, ask hotel personnel how long it may take to reach your destination. Make sure you tell them the time of your appointment. If you are driving to a studio, ask the people you are meeting if you will need a "drive-on" pass, which entrance you should use, and where you are supposed to park.

If you are not driving, be sure to pre-order a taxi. Allow extra time so you can arrive at your destination without fear of being late.

If you are coming from out of town and must either fly or drive in and out of the area on the same day, it is best not to schedule your appointment before 11:00 a.m., if you have a choice. Airports and freeways in Los Angeles County are notoriously congested until 9:30 or 10:00 in the morning. Also, it is not unusual for many producers and execs to start their days with breakfast meetings that keep them out of the office until mid to late morning.

If you have a choice, try not to schedule a meeting at the very end of a work day (after 6:00 p.m.). There are three reasons for this strategy: One is that the typical workday gets busier as the hours stretch on and, by the end of the day, the producer or the exec may be overwhelmed. Second, if any of the meetings scheduled ahead of yours are running late, everything else on that person's agenda will also be running late. And finally, if you have a plane to catch or a dinner appointment to keep, you may be feeling somewhat restricted and stressed.

Last but not least, always call ahead to confirm a meeting.

LOOK THE PART

While there is no formal dress code in Hollywood, it is best to wear neat, presentable, comfortable clothing. For men, slacks or casual pants and a collared shirt are appropriate. Polo-style shirts or short-sleeved shirts are fine. Suits and ties, for the most part, are not really necessary and are seldom worn for pitch meetings. For women, slacks or a skirt with a blouse or a sweater are fine, as is a casual dress. Shorts, tank tops, sweats, or revealing outfits — no matter how comfortable — are not the best clothing choice.

Do not forget to bring along a pen and a pad of paper to jot down any notes if you do not trust your memory. Unless you have gotten permission in advance, it is best not to bring along a cassette recorder. If you will be pitching a project (or if you think there is a remote possibility you might be), bring along note cards outlining your pitch if you think you will need them. And, remembering the lessons of Chapter 3, you might bring a P.O.P. to leave in case the potential buyer is interested.

Suppress the urge to bring along a camera. Most studios will not allow them on the lot anyway. Also, be aware that once you have entered the gates of the studio, you are on private property. Security personnel can request and legally have the right to look into briefcases, backpacks, purses, and the trunk of your car.

BE PROMPT, PATIENT, AND FLEXIBLE

When you arrive at the studio or the production company, the receptionist or the security personnel will ask your name, the name of the person you are meeting, and the time of your appointment. While it is wise to arrive slightly early or at least on time, do not be surprised if your meeting does not start right when scheduled. It is not uncommon for producers or execs to get tied up in other meetings or stuck on important phone calls. Use the wait to read the trades which are usually sitting nearby. These newspapers can give you additional up-to-the-minute industry information for "small talk."

While a producer or an exec may not have mentioned it, do not be surprised if there is another creative exec or development associate included in your meeting. Usually this person will be responsible for writing up any ideas you pitch. Producers and executives sometimes schedule multiple pitch meetings a day, and it can be difficult to remember who pitched what when 6:00 p.m. rolls around.

From a potential buyer's point of view, it is helpful to have another person listening to a pitch, especially if the project being considered is a comedy or is of a very specific genre. What may make you laugh may go over the head of someone else, so with an additional person in the room, the better the chances are that a comedy will be well received. The same is true if a sci-fi, fantasy, or unusually complicated project is being discussed. The more "ears" hearing your idea, the better the chances are that your project will appeal to at least one of the persons receiving your pitch.

RELAX AND CHAT
Most meetings start off with the usual introductory patter: Where do you live? Did you go to film school? How did you get started in writing? Producers/execs will often ask about your favorite movies, hobbies, books, etc. While some of this is "getting to know you," your hosts may file away the information for future reference. And that can pay off:

I once asked a writer what he did in his spare time and discovered he was a baseball fanatic who was an avid participator in fantasy leagues. Several weeks later, my studio was looking for someone to do a rewrite on a baseball project we had in development, and that writer turned out to be the first one we considered for the assignment.

GETTING DOWN TO BUSINESS

There will almost always be a few words about your script. The producer has read it and will probably tell you what she liked most about your story or the writing. If the company is interested in buying or optioning your script, she will usually let you know at the top of the meeting.

If you have an agent, a manager, or an entertainment attorney who represents you, the producer or the executive will probably have discussed this possibility in advance. Hopefully, your representative has informed you about this likelihood as well. Negotiating, however, is usually done by the agent, and not during your meeting with the buyer. In fact, in most cases, negotiating directly with a writer can be considered "poor form." Most producers or execs would prefer having these discussions with the writer's representative if possible, so as not to "sour" the solid working relationship that must exist, should they be producing your script. This approach is called keeping the deal "pure."

If you do not have an agent, listen carefully to everything that is said. Take notes if you like. Most producers/execs will ask you upfront if you are represented by an agent or an entertainment attorney. Let them know that you are "in the process of finding representation." If you feel comfortable with them by the end of the meeting, you might want to ask if they would be willing to recommend a reputable agent by making a call or letting you use their names as a referral.

Please note that you are under absolutely no obligation to sign with anyone the producer recommends, but it is always worth pursuing a personal recommendation in Hollywood; such recommendations should not be taken lightly. And remember that having a producer or a studio interested in purchasing or optioning your material is a "door opener" for getting an agent to look at your work and possibly represent you.

Use Your Opportunities
If the meeting is a "look-see" (most meetings in Hollywood are informational rather than deal-making) and if an opportunity presents itself, you can give a one-minute pitch (an expanded logline) of a project you think might be appropriate for the company or the studio. It is up to you to judge whether a genuine opportunity exists.

If you are not certain, you might want to ask the producer or the exec if you can schedule a pitch meeting in the near future. If, however, the exec seems interested and asks you to continue, give your five-minute pitch. If the exec is still interested, he will probably ask if you have completed the screenplay. If you have, you can leave a copy (be sure it is registered with the Writers Guild). If you do not have an agent, you should ask for a release form at this point. If you do have an agent, let the potential buyer know that the agency will send a copy of the script if you do not happen to have a copy with you.

If the screenplay is not completed, let the exec know what stage it is in — outline, treatment, partial script, etc. — and give a ballpark completion date. It is up to you if you wish to leave a P.O.P. Most writers feel more confident leaving a self-written pitch than relying upon a creative exec to write up his version of your idea.

Do not be afraid to ask what kinds of projects the company is interested in doing or if the studio has development deals with any particular acting or directing talent. This information can prove invaluable to you in the future and gives you an idea of the direction and the needs of the company or the studio. Asking questions also implies genuine interest.

FILL IN THE BLANKS

Most look-see and pitch meetings last about half an hour. Once the meeting is completed, take the time for a breather and treat yourself to a cup of tea or coffee. Go over your notes, filling in other details you feel are important. If you have an agent, give her a call to describe how the meeting went. If you pitched a specific project, left any written material, mentioned a project in the works, or promised to send a copy of your material, it is important to inform your agent so she can follow up at the appropriate time.

Some writers keep a log of meetings, recording the day, date, time, and place of each appointment, as well as the names of the studio or the production company personnel with whom they met. Details of any information gathered from the meeting and the reactions to any projects mentioned or pitched should also be noted. This log can be very helpful in establishing a "paper trail" of your project, as well as a "refresher" to remind you of anything which needs follow-up.

Follow Up

A day or two after the meeting, you may want to send an informal note to the person with whom you met. Thank the producer or the exec for meeting with you to discuss your work and mention the title of the project(s) you pitched or discussed. If the producer or the exec was especially helpful (in recommending an agent, suggesting a more appropriate contact for one of your projects, or giving constructive criticism or praise for your work), mention this in your note.

If you told the exec about any work in progress, you can close your note by saying something along these lines: "I'm halfway through my latest thriller, which should be completed within the next month or so. The story has a strong female lead and since Actress X has a production deal with your company, the script might fit nicely into your development slate." In this way, your thank-you note serves a dual purpose: to thank the producer or the exec and to give you the opportunity for an invitation for more work and meetings in the future.

If your meeting goes well, it will probably be the first of many. Whether your first meeting results in a sale or not, it can be the start of a potentially productive business relationship.

PART III – SUBMISSIONS: WHAT TO DO
AND WHAT NOT TO DO

CHAPTER 6

MAKING A LIST AND CHECKING IT TWICE — A 10-POINT CHECKLIST FOR A COMPLETED SCRIPT

You have read all of Linda Seger's books*. You have probably taken at least one or two workshops or a couple of courses on screenwriting through your local university or college. You have finally mastered the art of proper margin settings and scene headings. And you have typed, at last, those long-awaited words, "FADE OUT" — indicating the completion of your script.

Now, take a deep breath and consider your answers to the following important questions before sending your script to Steven Spielberg.

1. ARE MY CHARACTERS WELL-DRAWN AND INTERESTING?
Your characters are responsible for telling your story. Along the way, it is vital that they also capture our interest and sympathy. Your hero or heroine should be vulnerable and relatable, as well as courageous. You show these traits by putting your main character through a series of tests in which he or she may sometimes fail but will ultimately succeed.

---

*Making A Good Script Great, Creating Unforgettable Characters and The Art of Adaptation: Turning Fact and Fiction into Film are among my favorites.

These tests can be physical and/or emotional in nature and serve as plot complications.

EXAMPLES:

- Tom Hanks' character overcomes both grief and distance in *Sleepless in Seattle*.

- Scarlett O'Hara overcomes her self-centered ways and the horrors of the Civil War in *Gone With The Wind*.

The physical and the emotional journey your hero or heroine takes (and the lessons learned along the way) is what is commonly referred to as a **character arc**.

While most writers spend a great deal of time and energy breathing life into their hero or heroine, not nearly enough development goes into their villain and secondary characters. Bad guys and sidekicks are every bit as important as the hero to give your story the texture and the tone that can set it apart from all the rest.

EXAMPLES:

- Where would Luke Skywalker be without Darth Vader to put him to the test in *Star Wars*?

- And who can forget the villainy of the Sheriff of Nottingham, who vowed to put an end to *Robin Hood*?

Secondary characters give us important backstory on the hero and the situation at hand. They often provide vital information which helps to advance the plot. They help to define the goals of the hero and often will be involved in a minor subplot which complements and supports the movie's main theme. Secondary characters can also provide comic relief and a contrast to the hero's personality.

EXAMPLES:

- Would Ariel still be voiceless without the loyalty and the friendship of Flounder and Sebastian in *The Little Mermaid*?

- Would Alex Foley have been as successful in rounding up the bad guys without the help and the support of straitlaced, by-the-book officers Taggart and Rosewood in *Beverly Hills Cop*?

2. DOES MY DIALOGUE ADD TO THE PERSONALITY OF MY CHARACTERS AND SUPPORT THE PLOT POINTS OF MY STORY?
Your dialogue should be meaningful and appropriately "in character" with the personality of each role you have created. It should effectively convey the thoughts and the feelings of your characters and reveal any plot points that are key to the progression of the story. All of this should be done, however, in a subtle, natural-sounding way.

Now is the time to go through your script with a mental red pen to make sure each line and each word is absolutely necessary. It is especially important that each character has his own voice. Here are three simple, but effective, ways to test your dialogue:

- Cover up the names above the dialogue and see if each of your characters is easy to distinguish from the others. Remember that your dialogue should be consistent with the personality of each individual.

- Ask your major characters the same question and see if you can give each answers that readily separate them from one another.

- Ask members of your writing group or close friends to act out a scene or two. Hearing "lines" spoken out loud can be quite an eye opener for a writer and is a very effective method to quickly pinpoint any dialogue trouble spots.

3. DOES MY STORY FALL WITHIN A GENERAL THREE-ACT STRUCTURE?

Many new scripters are intimidated by the term "three-act structure." Have no fear, writers, all we are talking about is a beginning, a middle, and an ending. All stories (short stories, plays, novels, and motion pictures) have the same classic structure. Take a look at the basic three-act structure using the film *Witness* as an example:

- Your "beginning" should have an attention-getting setup that introduces your characters and their dilemma.

EXAMPLE:
Dedicated POLICE OFFICER finds his life in jeopardy when a young AMISH BOY identifies the officer's BOSS as the man behind a drug-related murder.

- Your "middle" should have character dynamics, action, and plot complications that both entertain and involve the audience as the story progresses.

EXAMPLE:
The OFFICER is forced to seek refuge in the peaceful Amish community where he is attracted to the recently-widowed MOTHER of the young AMISH BOY. The OFFICER finds himself at odds with, but gradually adapts to, the gentle ways of the community. Unfortunately, his BOSS soon discovers his hiding place, putting the Amish community at risk.

• And your "ending" should be compelling and satisfying by wrapping up all major and minor plot points and character relationships in a memorable way.

EXAMPLE:

The OFFICER is confronted at gunpoint by his BOSS and nearly killed, but the Amish community surrounds the two men and "bears witness," forcing the surrender of his BOSS. The Officer and the AMISH WIDOW have a bittersweet farewell, knowing their worlds are far too different to compromise.

4. DOES EACH SCENE HAVE A DISTINCT PURPOSE FOR BEING INCLUDED?

Time to get out that mental red pen again and selectively excise any scenes which are affecting the pace of your story and slowing down your plotline. Many a novice scripter can be easily identified by a screenplay weighed down by extraneous sequences and conversations which go on a beat or two longer than necessary.

If your script weighs in over the unspoken 120-page "line of demarcation," you might want to combine scenes if possible.

EXAMPLES:

• Your script contains a series of scenes in which the hero learns two pieces of information. Would your story be just as effective by merging two of the scenes into one?

• Your screenplay includes a small scene between the heroine and her mother to show they do not get along. Could that information be included in another conversation your heroine has with her best friend, who already plays a more significant role throughout the overall story?

5. HAVE I PAID ATTENTION TO DETAILS BY DOING PROPER RESEARCH?

If your story is set in a specific area, foreign country, or unusual environment, take the time to read about that location before attempting to recreate it on the page. If your story takes place during a particular historical period, go to the library, surf the Internet, or speak at length with an authority on that era for detailed information or little-known, but interesting anecdotes that can add color and atmosphere. Information on such subjects as politics, religion, clothing, music, architecture, modes of transportation, women's roles in society, education, issues of the time, etc., can provide valuable observations on what life was like and can add to the challenges of your characters and the conflicts they are facing.

A word of caution, however: Try to suppress the urge to go overboard by showing off too much of your newly-acquired knowledge. Do not allow those descriptive paragraphs to become so heavily detailed that they overshadow your story and bog down the pace.

If your movie project takes place in an unknown or futuristic world, be sure to take the time to map out the geographical, political, cultural, economical, social, and familial details of this new environment in a concise, but stylized manner.

Whether your story takes place in the past, the present, or the future, one of your primary concerns is to immediately immerse your potential buyer or agent into the "world" of your movie project. Familiarizing the reader is what is commonly known as **setting the scene**. The sooner your reader becomes comfortably "oriented" with your story's surroundings, the sooner he will be "hooked" into your project.

6. DO I KNOW WHO MY TARGET AUDIENCE IS?

Ideally, all writers would like the whole world to see their movies, but the simple truth remains that not all stories will appeal to everyone. If your goal is to sell your screenplay as a motion picture project, you should find out what other successful films fall into the same category as your script. After finding other movies that fall under the same general genre, you should ask yourself the following:

- What was the predominant age range of the audience viewing these similar films?

- Was it predominantly a male or a female audience?

- Did these films have considerable crossover appeal? In other words, did they attract the interest of a wide range of individuals by crossing sexual, socioeconomic, racial, cultural, and age lines?

- Which studio or production company distributed and/or produced these films? Do you remember how the films were promoted, i.e., what was the emphasis, theme, or main thrust of the trailers, television promos, and print ads?

It is important to keep in mind that not all movies are meant to be produced and distributed by large studios. Many successful films have been made and distributed by smaller independent companies who specialize in less commercial fare.

By knowing who your target audience is, you will have a much more realistic idea of which production companies or distributors to target when you are ready to start submitting your material. If you have not already done so, I urge you to invest in the *Hollywood Creative Directory's Producers*. If your local bookstore does not have it, you can call the publishers directly: In California, call (310) 315-4815; outside California call (800) 815-0503. Or you can contact them at their Web site: *www.hcd.com*. The directory contains the addresses, Web sites, and phone and fax numbers of more than 2,000 production companies, networks, cable entities, and studios.

More important, the *Hollywood Creative Directory's Producers* contains a partial listing of produced credits and the names and the titles of each company's executives. From these listings, you can easily eliminate those companies which may not be appropriate for your low-budget horror script or your historical drama, and you will be able to more effectively pinpoint your query by directing it to the appropriate person in charge (usually a creative exec, director of development, story editor, or vice president of production).

Needless to say, "targeting" can save a writer considerable time and effort, not to mention the costs of phone calls, postage, envelopes, and duplication of scripts.

7. HAVE I STREAMLINED MY STORYTELLING?
Nothing slows down the reading of a script more than extraneous material. Writers should always focus on writing the best story possible; yet many writers become so involved in detailing their film *exactly* as they have always envisioned it, they clutter up their efforts and end up slowing down the pace of their storytelling. Here are some tips to help you streamline your script:

- Keep camera angles and descriptive paragraphs to a minimum — even if you are attempting to faithfully adapt a novel. Screenplays of today are lean. They contain very few specific camera angles and descriptive paragraphs are concise, giving just enough information to set the scene and/or the atmosphere.

- Remember to break up any action description so it is not one massive block of words. Describing an action sequence in a series of two or three sentence paragraphs is much easier to read and gives the potential buyer a feeling of anticipation or urgency, as well as movement.

- If possible, eliminate all flashbacks and voiceovers or keep them to an absolute minimum. In addition to the extra expense of more sets, props, costumes, stuntwork, and actors, flashbacks — if overused and not judiciously placed — can be confusing to the audience. Voiceover is a device that is generally ineffective unless it is used in a highly stylized manner. Nostalgic film projects can sometimes benefit from a few well-placed voiceovers.

EXAMPLES:
- In the television series *The Wonder Years*, the voice of an adult Kevin sets the scene or conveys his glee, embarrassment, or adolescent angst OFF CAMERA, as Kevin (the kid) is shown ON CAMERA, carrying out the story.

- In the movie *Stand By Me*, Richard Dreyfuss' adult voice as Gordon is heard as he sets the stage for an important turning point in his adolescent life (when his character is played on screen by the young Wil Wheaton).

8.   CAN I SUMMARIZE MY STORY IN ONE OR TWO SENTENCES?
When queried by agents or execs, the experienced writer can usually summarize her script with just a few brief sentences, while writers who are less experienced have been known to go on for more than ten minutes or ten pages "summarizing" their movie. To encapsulate the essence of your story, create a logline. Think of a logline as a slightly expanded *TV Guide* blurb that summarizes the Movie of the Week or the latest episode of your favorite weekly television series.

Your logline must tease the potential buyer, making him want to hear more of the story. In the following example of developing a logline for *Beverly Hills Cop*, notice how each succeeding version adds more intrigue and builds in importance:

- Cop investigates killing — We know what the main character will be doing during most of the movie.

- Cop investigates killing of best friend — We now know that the main character will have a personal stake in the investigation.

- Detroit cop travels to Beverly Hills to investigate the death of his best friend — We are aware that the main character, who is from Detroit, will probably be a "fish-out-of-water" during his investigation in Beverly Hills.

- Street-wise Detroit cop turns Beverly Hills upside down to uncover the man responsible for killing his best friend — We have an indication that the main character is not only determined, but probably used to dealing with an investigation in an unorthodox manner. In fact, this final logline gives us the distinct feeling that there are going to be a lot of "fireworks" as he doggedly pursues this case to avenge the murder of his best friend.

As in the above example, it is often helpful to start out with a skeletal one-sentence summation, then build upon it. Do not forget to use those verbs, adjectives, and adverbs to add color, personality, and attitude to help sell your project. Here are two more examples of loglines from successful films:

- An extraterrestrial is accidentally stranded on earth and must depend upon his extraordinary friendship with a young boy to find his way home (*E.T. the Extra-Terrestrial*).

- Following the Civil War, a soldier is assigned to a remote prairie outpost where he forges a deeply spiritual bond with his Sioux neighbors (*Dances With Wolves*).

9. IS MY SCREENPLAY IN PROFESSIONAL SHAPE FOR SUBMISSION?
Much of this information might sound like simple common sense, but form is the one area which can be an overlooked downfall for a novice writer. Here is a checklist:

- All scripts should be cleanly typed or printed, with absolutely no handwritten notations. Remember to use an easy-to-read typeface or font, preferably in 12 pitch.

- Your screenplay should be carefully proofread for grammatical errors, improper punctuation, and misspelled words and typos. If you belong to a writing group, offer to trade off proofreading duties with another member or ask a friend who excels in English.

- Be sure your screenplay is copied onto plain white bond — absolutely no colored pages, onionskin, or parchment.

- You should always submit a copy and never an original of your script.

- Place your script in three-hole punched card stock covers, fastened with two brads that are long enough to hold the script securely. Most screenplays are submitted without a title on the card stock cover, but if you want to invest in having the title neatly printed onto the front cover, you can do so.

- There should be a title page listing the title of your script and your name as the writer. If you are not represented by an agent, you may put "Registered with the WGA" (if the script is) near the bottom. You should also add an address, phone number, and e-mail information so Hollywood knows how to contact you. There is no need to add the registration number or a "warning." If your script is not registered with the Writers Guild of America, I suggest doing so. Registration is currently $20 for nonmembers; the WGA can be reached at the numbers listed on page 25 for more detailed information on the registration process.

- Be sure you have numbered each page in the top right-hand corner, and again, please do not number scenes. After making copies of your screenplay, be sure to check for any missing pages. Nothing is more frustrating or annoying to a potential buyer (and possibly damaging to your chances for a sale) than coming to an important or crucial part of a story only to find a page or two are missing.

If you have followed the checklist on the preceding pages, as well as the guidelines for standard screenplay formatting, you should be in good professional-looking shape. One of the most reliable references for screenplay formatting is *The Screenwriter's Bible* by David Trottier. The WGA also puts out a brief, concise pamphlet on formatting. You can contact the WGA for details on obtaining this helpful booklet.

10. IS THIS A STORY THAT I LOVE?

My advice to new writers is to make your script a story that you love. It does not have to be a story that is commercial, but it should be well written. Few writers sell their first script, but the first few scripts can signal an agent that you are a writer who is consistent, determined, and passionate.

In speaking with scores of successful screenwriters through the years, I have discovered that it takes an average of seven to eight scripts before a writer obtains her first agent or has her work optioned or purchased. Only one writer sold her very first script and she was quick to add that it took her five more years before she had another sale. Another screenwriter wrote fifteen scripts before he got an option; he confided, in hindsight, his first ten screenplays are now an embarrassment to him, but were necessary practice.

It is also important that new scripters understand that most potential buyers are looking at screenplays with two key questions in mind:

- Is this a project that is appropriate for my company?

- Is this a writer that warrants a spot on my Writers List for future projects and rewrites?

Many times I have read a screenplay which was not appropriate for the studio where I was employed, but the writing was so impressive that I put the writer on a list for upcoming open writing assignments.

Keep in mind that each of your screenplays should be a labor of love that exhibits strong writing and storytelling skills. That effort can translate into a "calling-card" script which will open the doors for future work.

Some words of wisdom: Once you have completed a script, immediately suppress the urge to rest on your laurels. After a congratulatory sip of champagne or designer water, get to work on your next screenplay. Agents and production execs just love doing business with fast, prolific, creative talent!

CHAPTER 7

THE SUBMISSION AND DEVELOPMENT PROCESSES — WHAT HAPPENS TO A SCRIPT ONCE IT IS SUBMITTED AKA WHO IS READING MY SCRIPT AND WHAT ARE THEY LOOKING FOR?

Undiscovered scripters are always wondering, "What happens to my screenplay once it is submitted?" Contrary to popular belief, screenplays do not fall into a "black hole." But the submission process — often long and tedious — can try the souls of even the most patient of writers. Let's walk through the typical process.

AT THE START

If you have a Writers Guild of America-approved agent, he will submit your script to an independent production company or studio. Most major production companies and studios have very strict submission policies, controlled by their legal departments, for all screenplays, teleplays, treatments, novels, and other submitted materials. In most cases, they will accept material only from a WGA-accredited agent, a producer with a viable track record, or an entertainment attorney. Unsolicited material is generally verboten.

As mentioned previously, non-represented writers have been known to persuade a smaller independent production company to look at their scripts after they have agreed to sign a release form (see page 190 for an in-depth explanation of these forms).

Unless you have a contact who has expressed interest in the project at a particular studio, concentrate on finding a home for your script with a production company. Generally, producers are more willing to champion a project. In addition, if a screenplay has been submitted to a studio in recent years, the chances are there is a record of the submission, along with the coverage on it. Accordingly, producers will usually query a writer to find out if she has had the screenplay submitted to the studio beforehand. If it has been submitted to Studio X, the project is likely to be dismissed out of hand even if it has been revised.

Here's another very good reason why you should find a home for your project with a producer: Studios know that producers have taken the time to sift through hundreds of scripts before finding just the right project. They realize that the producer has a vested interest in the script and, more importantly, has most likely established a good working relationship with the writer.

THE LOG-IN

Once your screenplay reaches a producer or a studio executive, it is likely that he will give it to the story department for what is commonly referred to as the **log-in**, the producer's or the studio's legal record of material which has been submitted. All available information is recorded: the title of the project; the writer's name; if the material is based on previous material (i.e., a book, article, play, etc.); the name of the agent, entertainment attorney, or producer submitting/representing the project; what form of material (script, book, treatment, etc.); the page count; the date the material is received; and the name of the production company or studio personnel to whom the project is submitted.

The story department will then check its files to see if the material has ever been submitted and evaluated previously. Story department files often go back decades in time. With the advent of computer programs, it is very easy to crosscheck a project, not only by title, but also by the author's name. It is not unusual for writers or agents to change the title of a screenplay in hopes of receiving "new" coverage. Generally speaking, if a project received previous coverage, the story department will send that coverage to the exec. It is then up to the exec to decide if new coverage is warranted.

Some possible factors which may warrant that new coverage be given include: a significant difference in the page count from the original material (usually indicative that more than cosmetic or minor changes have been made), a letter from the producer or the agent which indicates a totally new approach to the project, or an indication from the producer or the agent that a major director or actor is now attached to the project.

THE GATEKEEPERS

In most cases, your script goes to a **reader** or **story analyst** whose job is to thoroughly read and evaluate your project. One studio head has described story analysts as the "gatekeepers."

Although it may sound unkind, producer and studio execs do not have sufficient time to read each and every piece of material which is submitted to them. In fact, at the most, execs will only read submissions from writers who have a track record in the industry or whose work is submitted by a high-profile producer.

This process may seem unfair, but the average studio receives between 800 to 1,000 screenplays every month from agents, producers, and entertainment attorneys — not including a large number of unsolicited projects which are generally returned by the mail room and never reach the desk of a studio exec or the story department. It would be virtually impossible for a handful of executives to read and evaluate all unsolicited material and still have time to work with writers on developing purchased scripts while shepherding dozens of projects through the never-ending production pipeline.

If your material is submitted to a studio, it will be read by a story analyst who belongs to the Story Analysts Guild, which is now under the umbrella of the larger Film Editors Guild. In general, union story analysts are better paid and enjoy better benefits than their freelance brethren who usually work for the production companies and the agencies. It is not unusual for freelance readers to work for more than two or three production companies to earn a livable salary. Most agency readers, however, are not allowed to work for other production companies or agencies.

Readers who work for agencies are usually planning to move up and become agents and producers. Analysts at the studios are occasionally promoted to become part of the creative group, which makes the decisions on the films that will be developed and produced. Readers for production companies often use their position as a stepping stone to move up to become part of the company's production staff.

Story analysts/readers vary in skills and abilities, but all are required to read, evaluate, and write up a report, called **coverage**, on submitted material. More experienced union story analysts are often called upon to do **development notes**, which are detailed comments and specific suggestions for projects the company has already optioned or purchased. And there is a small cadre of story analysts who are sometimes called upon to do "legal comparisons" in connection with a potential or pending lawsuit or infringement of rights. A very small number of story analysts are also trained to do foreign translation of scripts.

Both union and non-union readers are occasionally requested to sit in on pitch meetings where they are to take notes and write up a brief summary of the pitch. Readers often do more than simply read. Some are also asked to watch and evaluate student films and director's reels or films submitted for acquisition and distribution. Again, a synopsis and brief commentary is written up and serves as a report to executives who were unable to attend the screenings.

A READER'S CRYSTAL BALL

What do story analysts, producers, or studio execs look for in scripts? First, they look for projects they would like to make that would be appropriate for their studio or company. Second, they assess if the writer demonstrates strong enough storytelling skills and is someone they may want to do business with in the future.

In general, studios and production companies rely upon story analysts to look for the following:

- An unusually compelling basic plot that will fit into and balance the company's or the studio's existing development slate

- A project that has a certain amount of commercial potential that will attract a fairly large number of moviegoers

- Riveting, unique, but believable character dynamics that will attract a wealth of casting possibilities

- Fresh, insightful dialogue that adds to the backstory and the personality of the characters while moving the storyline along

- A keen visual and emotional storytelling style that can be "seen" while the analyst is reading the material

- The potential for a project that would be appropriate for any directors or acting talent who have a strong connection with the studio or the production company

- An exceptionally talented writer who can be put on the Writers List for possible rewrites or to write a script from scratch based on an in-house idea

THE COVERAGE REPORT

Coverage is a shorthand report that is an essential tool in this highly-competitive, but lucrative and busy marketplace. Coverage gives the time-conscious executive a concise, accurate (albeit, sometimes sterile) retelling of the main storyline and sub-plots, accompanied by comments on the material and the writing style. The average coverage is usually between one to three pages in length.

After reading your material, analysts will write a logline, followed by a synopsis of the storyline, noting major characters and plot points. Synopses can be as brief as a couple of paragraphs or as long and detailed as prescribed by the producer or the studio exec.

The synopsis is usually followed by a commentary which details the material's strengths and weaknesses, with additional remarks about the writer's abilities and writing style, and reasons why the story did or did not work. Finally, there is an evaluation: Pass, Consider, or Recommend. Many studios/production companies also have "box scores" which rate various aspects of the material, such as premise, story line, structure, characterization, dialogue, etc. A box score can range between "excellent," "very good," "fair," and "poor."

Short coverage is usually a one to one-and-a-half page synopsis with commentary. **Long coverage** is much more detailed and usually consists of more than three pages of synopsis and commentary. Long coverage is sometimes requested, especially if the analyst is evaluating a novel. If the material is being covered for an agency or for a production company whose principal is an actor or a director, it is not unusual for the reader to also do what is commonly referred to as a "character breakdown."

Character breakdowns generally accompany a detailed synopsis and commentary and also contain a list of the major roles with descriptions noting age range, physical aspects, personality, character arcs, interaction with other characters, and any significant traits which would give the studio exec, the production exec, or the agent a better idea of the casting possibilities.

Coverages of screenplays, novels, pitches, films, and other materials also serve as an accurate accounting of what, where, when, and to whom the project was submitted, should a lawsuit arise.

THE EXECUTIVE SUITE

Readers will then return the submitted material, along with the completed coverage, to the story department. The department will then note the date the coverage has been turned in. The material and the coverage are then sent to the executive or the

93

producer who originally requested the coverage. He, in turn, will read the report. Even if the rating is a "pass," some producers and execs will read sections of the script if the logline interests them. If your material gets a "consider" or a "recommend," the script will definitely be read.

If It Is a Thumbs Up...

If the producer or the exec reads the material and agrees with a "consider" or "recommend," he will present the material to others in the creative group for consideration. If the majority of responses are favorable, the original exec will check the company's development slate to see if the project will fit in — determining whether the company has too many projects in a particular genre and whether the project will meet the company's budgetary guidelines and marketing focus.

At a studio, marketing execs are occasionally asked for their opinions regarding the box-office outlook for the potential new project. They will look at the possible demographics, the commercial potential, and the ease of selling the project to the public. It is not uncommon for executives from the areas of casting and budgeting to also be called in to read the screenplay and give their opinions.

If the script meets the company's various criteria, a writer's agent or the producer who submitted the project will be contacted and the arduous process of negotiating either an outright sale or an option will begin. If the material was submitted to a production company, the producer will contact the writer and his agent. If the writer does not have an agent, it is strongly suggested that he secure the services of an entertainment attorney and/or an agent to handle the negotiations at this point.

IF IT IS A THUMBS DOWN...

If the story analyst's recommendation is to pass on your material and the producer or the exec agrees with the assessment after reading the report, your agent or the submitting producer will be contacted (usually by phone). At some companies, the actual material will be returned to the submitter. But with Hollywood being in an ecological mindset, the script will usually be put in a bin for shredding unless the submitting party specifically requests the return of the material.

A notation will be made by the story department regarding the date the script was returned to the submitter.

THE POSITIVE PASS

If a reader gives your script a pass, but is impressed by the quality and the style of your writing, the producer or the studio exec will usually read the screenplay. If she also likes your writing style, she will be more than willing to continue receiving material written by you and will give serious consideration to hiring you for any appropriate polishes, rewrites, or new idea assignments — thus the term "positive pass." A call will be placed to your agent, who will ask that you be kept in mind as a "writer for hire" on any upcoming projects or rewrites. Many writers have initially established themselves by polishing or rewriting material written by another writer or by writing a script based upon a producer's or studio's in-house idea.

THE WAITING GAME

Do not be discouraged if Michael Eisner or Sherry Lansing has not called your agent or your producer with an immediate response. So much material is submitted to each production company and studio that it can take anywhere from one to six weeks for sub-mission turnarounds. On rare occasions, it can even take up to two months, depending upon the backlog.

Major studios usually have staffs of from eight to fifteen story ana-lysts who read an average of seven to ten screenplays a week. Production companies and agencies usually have a smaller reading staff. You can do the math, but obviously, it can sometimes take a month or more for submissions to be covered. Producers/execs will sometimes ask that a submission receive **rush coverage**, which means they would like the material to be covered immedi-ately (usually within twenty-four hours). Other times they may request **priority coverage**, which means within the next few days.

Rush or priority status is usually given to projects that are "hot" (the submitting agent or the producer is distributing the material to several entities at once) or are written by a scriptwriter who has had several successful films under his belt.

THE CREATIVE GROUP
As mentioned above, the decisions about purchasing or optioning material is put in the hands of the creative group. This group was first discussed on page 14: At its top is the head of the motion pic-ture division of the studio. At a production company, it is the principal/owner of the company. Immediately under the head of the motion picture group is the senior or executive vice president of production. At a studio, there are at least one or two persons at this level. At a production company, there is usually only one.

Under the senior or executive vice presidents of production are the vice presidents of production. At a studio, there are at least two or three at this position. In a production company, there is usually only one. The directors of development (aka creative execs) are next in line. There are generally three or four execs at this level of the creative group. Some studios and production companies have a story editor whose job is to supervise the readers/story analysts and to facilitate the influx of work that flows between the executives and the gatekeepers. Some story editors are also asked for their input as part of the creative group.

The higher you are in the creative group, the more responsibilities you have and the more weight your opinion is given in determining the fate of a project.

THE DEVELOPMENT PROCESS

Once a script has been purchased, creative execs/directors of development are responsible for gathering the group's notes and comments and putting them into a document which will be given to the producer and the writer for discussion before the next revision of the screenplay begins. In addition to merging the thoughts of the creative group into a readable document, these development executives are also responsible for making sure the notes are not only clear and concise, but also well-put (i.e., said "in a nice way") so as to not upset any egos.

After a rough draft of the studio notes are assembled, one of the vice presidents or the senior or executive vice president who is assigned to the project will go over the notes and will edit them, if needed. The notes are then sent to the producer and the writer and the first of several development meetings will be set.

DEVELOPMENT HELL

Producers and writers have been known to call the whole process of constant notes, meetings, and revisions, development hell. In the 1980s (when development was first utilized), there was a tendency to micromanage each project and revision. It was not unheard of for development memos to sometimes exceed ten to fifteen pages. Nowadays, development documents are usually in the two- to five-page range.

After the producer and the writer have had a chance to digest the notes from the studio, they decide which points they do and do not agree with. They will often work out an alternate solution and present it to the studio's development team (the director of development and the vice president).

While every writer wants to defend his material (as is well within his rights), most also realize that compromises are usually in order. Here are some of the reasons why studios may request changes:

- They need to change certain aspects of the plot to keep the project within a reasonable budget.

- They are concerned with straying into an undesirable "ratings" area.

- They are concerned with offending or alienating a segment of the moviegoing public.

- They are trying to "woo" a particular star and would like the character and/or the storyline to be adjusted to the star's acting range.

- They are trying to attract a particular director and would like the script to be more in line with the director's talents.

- They are concerned about more common issues such as pacing, tightening up the plot, providing dialogue that more strongly supports the character's personality and intent, and making sure to enhance but balance all aspects of the project to make it as entertaining and attractive to potential moviegoers as possible.

Some projects only require one or two revisions, while others have been known to go through a dozen or more revisions, as well as several different writers. Contrary to popular belief, most producers and studios would actually prefer keeping the original writer on the project, but if, after a couple of revisions, the writer is unable to deliver a screenplay that is suitable, hiring another writer is sometimes the only possible solution.

This process seems rather unfair, but once a studio or a producer has purchased your script, it is legally in their possession and ownership; they are well within their rights to assign a new writer if they feel they need to do so. Studios and producers do not assign new writers capriciously. Keep in mind that with relatively few exceptions, you (as the writer of the original material) will still receive a writing credit should the project be produced. It may not, however, be a sole credit but a shared one.

RED LIGHT MOMENTS

Once a project is bought by a production company or a studio, the goal is to give the project a greenlight and have it produced. Yet, more than half the screenplays that are purchased do not end up on the big screen. This fact is one of the most puzzling and frustrating aspects of the film industry. Here are some possible reasons why a film may be "abandoned" (dumped altogether) or put into turnaround:

- A big-name actor or actress has decided not to do the project.

- A director has accepted another prime project he would rather do first.

- There has been a major change in upper management.

- The original executive who championed the project has found another position at an opposing company or has been fired or let go in a management shake-up.

- The studio feels that the project's window of opportunity has past in terms of public interest.

Members of the Writers Guild of America have expressed a desire to have the right to re-acquire the rights to their work, and the WGA and the Motion Picture Association of America are exploring this possibility and all that it implies.

CHAPTER 8

BEWARE OF THE BIG EIGHT — THE EIGHT MOST COMMON REASONS WHY A SCRIPT CAN BE REJECTED

An all too familiar discussion took place just recently while "doing lunch" with some of my industry colleagues. As we talked about the ever-crowded script market, our laments over the dearth of really good material seemed to fall into several areas of very similar complaints. Although there is a common misconception among writers that everyone in Hollywood only wants to say "no" to everything, I am here to tell you — unequivocally — that most of us prefer and actually love to say "yes."

Aside from wanting an agent or a producer to look at a writer's work, one of the most frequent questions I hear from scripters is: "Why are so many scripts rejected by Hollywood?"

This question prompted me to ask other executives, agents, and producers about their answers and observations on why an average of nine out of ten submissions fails to make even the "first cut" past the story analysts or readers. After an informal survey, it became quite apparent that the reasons for a "pass" seemed to fall into eight general categories. Let's focus on what I call The Big Eight.

101

1. THE SNAIL TRAIL/TANGLED YARN START

Nothing stops a producer or a studio exec faster than a script that fails to move within the initial 15-20 pages. Some writers become so determined to introduce their characters or go into very elaborate detail to describe the movie's location that they fail to hook the audience into the heart of the story by firmly establishing the plot in Act I.

A writer needs to put himself in the audience's $8.00 seat. If a film does not grab your attention within the first twenty minutes, wouldn't you have the urge to exit the theater and demand your money back?

Alas, the reverse is also true. If the movie has too many confusing and tangled pieces of plotting thrown into Act I, an audience will become restless and is bound to start asking too many unnecessary internal questions — questions that will tend to override the main thrust of the storyline and ultimately overshadow your characters and the establishment of their primary goals.

A studio or a production exec faced with a never-ending mountain of scripts to read will be sorely tempted to stop reading if Act I is either too plodding or too confusing. One result: the 30/10 read discussed on page 52. And I am sorry to report that — as submissions are on the increase — several of my colleagues have confessed that they have found it necessary to further streamline things down to a "10/10 read."

While studio story analysts are required to read every page of a submitted material per studio policy, that every-page policy does not always extend to studio execs or freelance readers at production companies. This situation can be disconcerting to a writer, especially if the rest of his project has all the prerequisites for a potentially good script.

2. THE ACT II DRAG AKA THE MID-STORY SAG

The most common plotting pitfall is allowing the pacing in Act II to slow to a near grinding halt. Most writers have carefully crafted their attention-getting setup and have envisioned the spine-tingling, spellbinding climax to their film, but often fail to give as much thought and consideration to the story that falls in between the beginning and the end. This problem is especially noticeable in action, adventure, thriller, or "on the road" tales where writers have been known to resort to a series of unimaginative, non-stop chase sequences or a montage of scenery shots or special effects imagery in order to fill the void, show the passage of time, and move their story along.

Unfortunately, the opposite effect seems to take place. The audience loses interest because they are not being given enough essential time investment in the hero's struggle to reach his ultimate goal. And in many cases, the challenges the protagonist faces are not sufficiently laid out to give Act II a feeling of escalating danger, excitement, or jeopardy. As a result, Act II unexpectedly becomes a huge lull.

It is up to you, the writer, to make sure that Act II is infused with as much creative style and plotting as you have invested in your dynamic setup and the resultant "happy ending." Act II is the best time for your audience to get to know your characters and, in turn, to support your hero's or heroine's final goal. This Act is also the ideal place to add motivation and backstory, two very subtle but key ingredients in giving your audience a hero they can root for. This root-ability factor gives the audience an emotional investment in your main character(s). Every scene in Act II should build in intensity and importance, and serve to catapult the audience in anticipation toward your Act III climax.

3. THE FRENZIED FINISH

Many writers toil through their scripts, only to suddenly panic when they realize they have arrived at page 100. Frantically, there is a mad dash to provide a non-stop finish for the final fade out. One common example of what I call "the frenzied finish" is the **explanatory ending**, where the hero sits everyone down and starts to explain everything — who, what, why, where, and how. While this technique may be used with some degree of success in occasional television series such as *Murder She Wrote* or *Diagnosis: Murder*, it seldom works for cable, network television, or theatrical movies.

A movie's ending should never feel rushed or contrived. The climax should always be satisfying. All plot points and character relationships should be resolved in a logical and, hopefully, entertaining fashion. And although you want to keep your audience guessing, no one appreciates a story where the ultimate villain or his underlying motive seems to come out of left field without an adequate setup beforehand to support and justify the final outcome.

Take sufficient care with Act III. Although it is usually somewhat shorter in page length than Acts I and II, your third act's final dozen or so scenes will leave the most lasting impression on your audience. And that last impression could generate either good or bad "word of mouth" on your movie. It is even more crucial to create a memorable and satisfying ending on the *reading* pages of the script, or it may never be bought and make that all-important transition to the screen.

4. The Same-O, Same-O Syndrome

In an effort to mimic other popular movies of the day, many writers feel the need to follow a specific story pattern ("formula") too closely. Their reasoning? If it was successful for a particular popular movie, it should work for their projects as well. Unfortunately, the resulting screenplay is usually put in the rejection pile because buyers see it as the "same old" story.

A successful screenwriter once told me: Think of your movie as a cake. Cakes have certain standard ingredients, like flour, eggs, and oil. But some look and taste better than others because their creators deviated from the recipe, adding new ingredients, omitting others, changing the proportions slightly, adopting new techniques, and experimenting with the presentation for an inventive, unique, and successful end product.

By infusing your script with innovative style, thoughtful but creative plotting, distinctive characters, and fresh dialogue, you, too, can go a long way in avoiding that feeling of sameness. Do not be afraid to add a few unique twists to your project or to add some unexpected but satisfying elements that will delight and surprise your audience.

Buyers realize that there are only so many basic storylines that have been utilized since the days of the cavemen, but when a writer submits a project with a protagonist or an antagonist who has a unique or intriguing point of view, you can be sure your project and your creative "take" on your character's perspective on life will put your script in the much-coveted 10% pile of "considers" or "recommends."

5. THE KNOW-IT-ALL/SLOPPY SAM STORYTELLER

Submissions that fall into this particular rejection category include scripts where the writer has selected an area of expertise and is determined to tell the readers everything he knows about the subject. The unfortunate result is that the storyline gets loaded with too many unnecessary details — details like the kind of design on the buttons on a Victorian gentleman's topcoat or the specific version of a jazz classic playing in the background of a scene. This sort of detail usually results in impeding the pacing of the story, undercutting the escalation of the plot, and taking away from the development of your characters.

So, unless those fancy Victorian buttons on the villain's topcoat can lead to his downfall or the specific version of that jazz classic is the key to solving your mystery, it really is best to keep such overly-researched details to an absolute minimum.

On the other hand, a common pet peeve among potential buyers is what I call "The Sloppy Sam Storyteller," a writer whose screenplay is lacking in key details and contains very little in the way of stylish, visual atmospherics or color. The Sloppy Sam Storyteller has not taken the time to do important research, has given inaccurate information, and/or provided his storyline with faulty or little substantive logic.

Simply putting "EXT. MANHATTAN – STREET" is not sufficient enough to make readers feel they are in Manhattan. One or two sentences is all that is needed to give us a more distinct feeling of whether we are in the ritzy Upper Eastside of Fifth Avenue, with Central Park to the west and snobby doormen guarding Fortune 500 residents in their penthouse co-ops, or in the dark, gritty, vermin-infested recesses and broken-dream alleyways of Alphabet City in Lower Manhattan.

The writer has to keep in mind that the audience has paid good money to be transported to the world where your characters will meet, confront, and be challenged by their demons and fears before fulfilling their dreams two hours later. If the world is unfamiliar (i.e., in another galaxy, in a past era, in the future, in a make-believe country), it is the writer's responsibility to not only layout that unfamiliar world, but to make the audience (and the potential buyer) believe in that world and the marvels and the dangers it may hold.

6. FLASHBACK/VOICE-OVER HELL

While this reason for a rejection is more often symptomatic of the novice writer, from time to time some experienced scripters have confessed that they, too, will become stumped on how to insert information or backstory into their scripts. In desperation, they will often turn to flashbacks or voice-overs to do their storytelling for them. Unfortunately, if not used properly and sparingly, flashbacks and voice-overs can end up sinking a movie by confusing an audience and sidetracking them from the main storyline.

As a nostalgic device, voice-overs can sometimes be appropriate and effective; remember how a voice-over helped to establish the multiple mother-daughter relationships among four families in *The Joy Luck Club*? Flashbacks and flash-forwards can also be effective as a stylized storytelling device, as was the case in the fairy-tale film, *The Princess Bride*, where the movie would cut back to Peter Falk, who was telling the story to his enthralled grandson.

If faced with the temptation to use a flashback, flash-forward, or voice-over, you should first consider reviewing your story to see if the information you are trying to relay can be cleverly inserted, perhaps via dialogue, into a meaningful but related conversation.

Another reason for the red flag on flashbacks is a financial one. Flashbacks often involve another period of time and can add appreciably to a film's budget in terms of sets, costumes, props, and additional acting talent.

7.   THE KITCHEN-SINK THEORY

It has been said that we cannot please all of the people all of the time, yet many scripters still insist on trying to accomplish this goal by putting everything but "the kitchen sink" into their film project — often just to prove their movie has "something for everyone."

This theory reminds me of a submission that was sent to a studio story department several years ago. The basic premise was: "A young couple falls in love and time travels to outer space." Yet within the 125 pages, the young couple sang their way out of an underwater prison ruled by misplaced inhabitants from Atlantis *and* had an out-of-body experience where mythical figures warned them that, like history, they were doomed to repeat their mistakes with disastrous results. They *also* found time to flee to a lost galaxy to find happiness, while helping the inhabitants of the galaxy uncover the secret to survival.

The screenplay's cover letter sincerely and proudly announced to all: "Here is a movie that will appeal to the masses." Sadly, the script's tone fluctuated wildly from outright melodrama to camp humor because the writer attempted to crowd way too many genres into one film: science fiction, fantasy, mythology, drama, comedy, musical, melodrama, mystery, and romance!

Even in the highly imaginative and often improbable world of moviemaking, we cannot expect the audience to take too many leaps of faith at one given time. It is wise to remember that the best and most memorable films usually involve either an ordinary person in an extraordinary situation (such as *Harry Potter and the Sorcerer's Stone*, *The Princess Diaries*, or *Cast Away*) or an extraordinary hero in an ordinary world (such as *Forrest Gump* or *Superman*).

8. THE YAKKETY-YAK TRAP

Executives, agents, and producers concur that dialogue is one of the key ingredients in the sale of most screenplays. Yet many writers get carried away, writing long, dramatic speeches for their characters, either to drive home a point or to convey a piece of plotting.

Another sign of what is known as The Yakkety-Yak Trap is the conversation that drags on much too long. When the page count starts to mount, the wise writer will carefully review his dialogue, vigilantly aware that lengthy discussions, meaningless speeches, and monologues seldom have a place in a *moving* picture.

Instead of talking about their feelings, is there some way that you can show your characters in action? The first few minutes of the movies *An Unmarried Woman* and *Witness* have no words, but the subtle play of movement and emotions on the faces of their characters speaks volumes as Jill Clayburgh comes to terms with the end of her marriage in the former, and Kelly McGillis struggles with her new widowhood and the care of her young son in the latter.

Always keep in mind that the most interesting and revealing conversations come *after* the initial small talk. Though reality has us starting a conversation with "Hi, how are you? How's the family?" and ending with "Goodbye. Take care, I'll see you around," what an audience really needs to hear is what falls in between — the meat of the conversation, with as little fat as possible. As they say in the Biz: "Show me, don't tell me."

PART IV – THINKING BEYOND THE SCRIPT: THE

ONGOING WORK OF A WRITER

TO HIS WORK AND RELATIONSHIPS

CHAPTER 9

WALKIN' THE WALK – CREATING OPPORTUNITIES FOR YOURSELF

A dozen Hollywood agents received a personally-addressed fax with the following message: "Per our conversation, I'm sending by courier the hot spec from the new writer we discussed. Let me know what you think." The fax was signed with an indecipherable scrawl. A script with the same message arrived at each agent's office later that day. The only way to contact the mysterious sender was to call the phone number on the last page of the script, which belonged to a very gutsy new screenwriter. Although most of the agents didn't appreciate being duped, one admitted he liked the scripter's high-concept thriller enough that he agreed to send it to half a dozen of his producing clients. If one of them wanted to take on the project, the agent would gladly represent the writer. None of the producers liked the script enough to make it one of their projects, but at least the writer got twelve top agents and six well-known producers to read his work!

SUNDANCE SCREENWRITING LAB NEARING DEADLINE

TOP SCREENWRITERS FETED AT MOONDANCE FILM FESTIVAL

FOUR WIN NICHOLLS FELLOWSHIPS

UCLA COMEDY COMPETITIONS AWARDS ANNOUNCED

SCRIPTWRITERS GAIN AGENCY REPRESENTATION THROUGH ONLINE NETWORK

The above are just a few of the headlines that have merited feature articles in the Hollywood trade papers throughout the past year. The headlines are yet another reminder of an alternate way in which a new or an emerging scriptwriter can break into the Biz and get his work noticed by the industry. Screenwriting competitions and fellowships are an excellent way to announce to the world that you have got "the write stuff." And with the Internet, writers have found a new tool to gain recognition and to market their work.

Let's start with the screenwriting contests and fellowships first. What is the difference between a scriptwriting competition and a fellowship program? Which contests are best to enter and why?

FELLOWSHIPS
Fellowships are usually scholarships that will enable new screen-writers to practice and polish their craft under the experienced and watchful tutelage of professionals in the entertainment industry. Some of the fellowships are for as short as six months, while others can be for as long as a year. Usually a specified amount of money is given to each "fellow" (recipient) which will

provide either full or partial support while the writer is learning the tricks of the trade as he fine tunes his craft. During their tenure as fellows, writers will work under the careful guidance and supervision of a development or creative group at a studio or with a producer and his staff of writers on a television series.

Some fellowships are specific — usually for either television or features. If they are for television, some fellowships are divided into drama or comedy development. Most fellowship entries are read by a team of creative executives and story analysts who work for the studio or the production company sponsoring the program. In addition to having his work evaluated on an industry level, the writer will have his style, his attention to character development and dialogue, and his professional work ethics assessed.

Once the fellowship entrants are narrowed down to a more elite pool, telephone calls are placed to the semifinalists. Each is given the news of his lucky status and is asked a variety of questions — first and foremost: If chosen, will the writer be able to drop what he is doing and move to the Los Angeles area for the duration of the fellowship training? Other questions are designed to determine the potential recipient's experience level as a writer, as well as his ability to adjust to such industry expectations as long hours, flexible schedules, and working with a variety of egos and personalities.

After the semifinalists have been interviewed, members of the creative group narrow the list to the writers they feel are not only the most talented, but also possess the determination, the drive, and the adaptability to make the most of the fellowship program.

During their tenure, fellowship recipients will work on both their own projects and a variety of in-house assignments. For a television fellowship, a writer will be assigned to a specific show to work with a staff of writers. If the fellowship is for motion pictures, the writer will usually be paired with at least one or two members of the film division's creative group (ideally a senior vice president and a director of development), where he will come up with potential ideas for new projects while receiving feedback on the development of his own projects.

In some instances, if a fellow and his contribution to the creative group is well-received, he may be given an opportunity to continue his fellowship for an additional six months or a year. And in some cases where the fellowship is for television, a successful recipient may end up being given an opportunity to write one or two episodes of a series for a coming season.

COMPETITIONS AND CONTESTS

Competitions can vary in considerably different ways. Some offer no more than a nice piece of paper declaring you the winner of the contest, while others may offer cash prizes, scriptwriting-related prizes (i.e., subscriptions to trade papers, screenwriting software, etc.), and other opportunities. Most of these contests are sponsored by writing organizations, universities, film commissions, film festivals, or production companies.

The persons judging these competitions can vary from local volunteers or interns to organization members and professionals in the entertainment industry. While it is quite common for local volunteers or organization members to judge the preliminary round of a contest, the best competitions to enter are those in which the final judges serve a professional capacity in either film or television, i.e., studio executives, producers, agents, script consultants, entertainment attorneys, development specialists, or screenwriters.

In competitions where there are several hundred or a few thousand entries, there are at least three or four rounds of judging; these multiple rounds can take several months. Writers who progress to the quarterfinals and semifinals are usually notified by mail or e-mail of their status (not necessarily the case in smaller contests). When the judging comes down to the finalists, those writers are notified of the date, the time, and the location where the winners will be revealed and introduced. In most cases, it is up to the finalist to pay for her own transportation and lodging to these events.

FEES

Take note. Most contests and fellowships usually require some sort of an entry fee — generally used to help defray the cost of such expenses as mailing, logging in material, copying, paying for visiting judges, and other administrative costs incurred in running such a contest. Fees can range anywhere from a mere $25 up to $100+, although most seem to hover closer to the $50 range.

Some contests, in an effort to avoid a last-day flood of entries, have utilized a multi-tiered fee system, whereby the earlier you submit your script, the less you pay. Note that no matter what the entry fee, some competitions have what is called an "entry cap" or limit on the number of entries they will allow to be entered into competition.

WHY SHOULD I ENTER?

Entering fellowships and/or competitions offer several benefits for the unproduced screenwriter:

- First, this is an excellent way to test the water and find out how others, especially those in the industry, will respond to your story and to your writing talent.

- Second, it can be a significant and ego-boosting way to gain recognition for your writing efforts. Every writer deserves to have her work validated.

- Third, depending on how prestigious the fellowship or the contest may be, your script may be read by agents, producers, or studio execs who are eager to find new clients, new projects, and new candidates for rewrites and in-house projects.

HOW DO I ENTER?

Here are some common-sense guidelines:

- Complete and polish your script. If you belong to a writing group, have a few members of your group read and proof your screenplay for professional appearance, content, and writing style. If you desire, you may want to get a professional critique to help you with a rewrite.

- Read, read, read! Read the trade papers (*The Hollywood Reporter* and *Variety*, for example). Nationwide writing organizations like the American Screenwriters Association or publications like *Writer's Digest* and *Writer's Aide* also feature news about scriptwriting contests. Both *The*

Hollywood Scriptwriter and *The New York Screenwriter* are monthly newsletters that routinely contain articles on upcoming fellowships, film festivals, and competitions. You may also want to check chat rooms devoted to screenwriting to find out what your fellow scripters know about upcoming contests.

- Make a list of the competitions and fellowships that most interest you. Carefully note their fees and deadlines. Unless you thrive on stress, it is advisable not to submit your material at the very last minute. Be sure to allow yourself plenty of time to realistically mull over and revise your work once it is nearly completed. New writers often have that uncontrollable urge to send out their material the minute they have typed the last "FADE OUT." Suppress that urge. Seasoned writers will tell you that writing "The End" is only the very beginning.

- Look over all rules and guidelines with a fine-tooth comb. Some contests and fellowships specify what they will or will not accept. For example, some contests are very specific and will accept only family-oriented scripts, or will exclude all teleplays, or will accept only screenplays in which a majority of the movie can be filmed in a particular state or location. Most competitions are for unproduced writers (those whose work has not been turned into a theatrical or a television film). A few competitions will accept scripts that have been optioned but not yet produced. Of special note for those who qualify are those fellowships or competitions that focus on encouraging minorities (i.e., women, writers of color, writers over forty). You may want to send a query letter if the guidelines

119

are not clear to you. If there is a phone number or a Web site, do not hesitate to contact the sponsoring company or organization for answers to any and all of your questions.

- Follow all instructions to the letter. If the competition asks for the first fifteen pages of your script and a two-page, double-spaced synopsis of the rest of your story, do not submit the first eighteen pages and a three-page, single-spaced synopsis. If the contest limits you to one script not to exceed 125 pages, do not send your 138-page screenplay. If the directions ask that you put only the title on the front page, do not be tempted to add your name. (Most competitions are deliberately judged "blind," so those reading the material will not be tempted to give preference to a writer they know.) If an SASE is requested, remember to include an envelope large enough and with enough postage to allow for the return of your material. In most cases, the sponsoring organization will *not* return screenplays. Fill out your entry form by printing all requested information legibly and completely.

One administrator for a well-known fellowship competition told me that she has had to routinely disqualify as many as 10 to 15 percent of the entries in the annual screenwriting program she oversees, simply because writers neglected to read and follow the directions carefully. Make sure you do not waste such a significant investment of time, talent, and money (for copying, postage, and entry fees), only to be disqualified for not following the instructions and the rules.

WHICH COMPETITIONS SHOULD I ENTER?
No matter how large or how small, all competitions have some importance and serve a common but vital purpose: to recognize

and herald the accomplishments of writers. Some writers prefer to start out by entering smaller, local contests where they can hopefully gain a bit more confidence before branching out into larger, international competitions. If you are interested specifically in a fellowship program but live outside the Los Angeles area, you will have to seriously weigh the possibility of moving to and living in the Los Angeles area for an extended period of time.

Being a finalist can bring instant recognition, especially if the judges are professionals in the entertainment industry and include agents, producers, or studio executives. Carefully check competition brochures and Web sites for an indication of how the final judging will be conducted. And do not be afraid to inquire if industry professionals will be part of the final judging process. Although the sponsors may not be able to tell you exactly who will be part of the final judging panel, you may want to ask for the names of past judges or at least for the names of the studios, production companies, or agencies for which they have worked. The answer should give you an excellent idea of the professional caliber that is associated with the contest.

THE BIG WAIT

Keep in mind that the number of script submissions for these competitions is usually quite high. The Nicholls Fellowship alone receives in excess of 3,500 entries every year, some from as far away as South Africa, Brazil, India, and Sweden. Reaching the semifinals or finals of the Nicholls competition is considered quite a coup, given the large number of entrants annually. The Walt Disney Company Screenwriting Fellowship Program receives more than 1,200 submissions yearly.

You should expect to wait anywhere from one to six months after the entry deadline before winners are announced; the actual time will depend on the number of entries received. If you have not heard from the sponsoring organization after a reasonable period of time, or if they do not have a specific date on their brochure or Web site to announce their winners, you may want to send a SASE requesting a list.

During the long wait, continue to work on your next television or motion picture project. You should also look ahead toward entering other competitions or applying for fellowships. While being a finalist or even a winner does not guarantee a lucrative writing career, it can be an all-important "door opener" toward obtaining an agent for your work or securing that coveted and rare opportunity to submit your material to a producer.

MAKING THE MOST IF YOU ARE A FINALIST

After the winners have been announced, most studios and production entities will assign at least one or two development or creative executives to read and evaluate the final submissions of most of the major competitions. This is also standard operating procedure with most of Hollywood's larger literary agencies, who will have a team of junior agents evaluate the work of the finalists.

If you are a finalist, consider contacting various agencies and production companies by mail. In the letter, mention your recent accomplishment, stating the genre, along with a two-sentence logline. It is not unheard of for many of the finalists of the major competitions to obtain agency representation and/or an option of their material at a production company — even if they do not receive the top prize.

USING THE INTERNET

The Internet is a new way of breaking into the entertainment arena. Unproduced directors-writers have featured five to fifteen minute **shorts** (short films) of their projects on the Web, a few of which have actually spurred production companies and agents to sign up these industrious and creative types. But there is a similar ratio of good to bad shorts on the Internet as there are good to bad scripts that are submitted to producers and studios. One out of every ten might have some merit. And one out of every ten of those may be given serious consideration for a sale or representation.

In addition to the shorts that have been shown online, there are numerous Web sites devoted to loglines, synopses, and sometimes even partial or entire scripts for others to read and potential buyers to seek out. While this method is certainly one way to get a writer's work "out there," there is also the danger of having that work exposed and possibly stolen, altered, or plagiarized.

Here are some considerations if you are thinking of using one of these script-market Web sites:

- Find out as much as you can about the person running the site. If there is an e-mail or snail-mail address or phone number, contact the person and ask for his background and a history of the company (if none is given on the site).

- What fees are being required for your work to be put on the Web site? How long will your work remain on the site? What are other similar sites charging?

- Is a hard copy of the listed projects being sent to reliable agents and production companies or are the Web site creators relying on industry personnel to stumble across their service? In what ways and using what methods are the owners marketing their site to the industry? Can they be found on the most popular search engines like Google, Yahoo, etc.?

• How long has the site been in business? Can it name some of the production companies and the agencies that regularly use the site?

• Does the site have links to other industry-related sites or writing organizations? Generally speaking, the more recognized and legitimate a Web site is, the more professional links or connections it will have to other film and television sites.

• Does the site have an industry professional who answers questions or is featured online? Again, if an executive, consultant, agent, or screenwriter in the Biz is featured, that usually indicates the site has been checked out by the studio, production company, or agency that employs the professional.

• What exactly is required of you, the writer, to have your work put online? Is it a logline of fifty words or less? Is it a three-paragraph synopsis of your work? Or is it your entire screenplay?

• What kinds of guarantees can the Web site give you regarding its security?

• What kinds of "success stories" can the site give you? Does the site regularly mention any of these stories?

- If you are a member of a large writers group or participate in one of the dozens of screenwriting chat rooms that have been formed online, ask if anyone is familiar with the sites you are considering and/or if anyone has had good or bad experiences utilizing any of them. You might receive a reliable recommendation!

CHAPTER 10

STAYIN' ALIVE — RESOLUTIONS TO KEEP YOU PRODUCTIVE AND CHALLENGED AS A WRITER

One of the most common laments among writers is "What do I do while waiting for my script to sell?" Aside from encouraging you to continue to work on your next project, keeping yourself productive and motivated at any stage of the writing game can be your biggest challenge. Here are some resolutions to keep you going, no matter if you are waiting for the big sale or just getting started "in the game":

WRITE EVERY DAY
Easier said than done, but a true writer really does write just about every single day. Set a goal for yourself. Make it a "do-able" goal, be it one scene a day, Act I of your selling synopsis, polishing your query letter, a detailed character breakdown, or the opening paragraph for setting the scene of your new screenplay.

When you do not feel motivated to work on your current project, brainstorm new ideas or write in your diary or journal. If you are traveling, describe in a paragraph the sights, the sounds, and the smells of the day.

Keep a pad (or notebook) and pencil handy — on your nightstand to record memorable dreams, by the phone and in your car to capture ideas that spring up while you listen to talkative relatives or wait in traffic.

Some writers are never without a mini-cassette recorder or their handheld organizers to record great notions for future projects or solutions to current ones. Inspirations, like opportunities, often come to us at the most unexpected moments — so be prepared to capture them.

START A MARKETING LIST

Find and pursue at least one or two marketing possibilities each week. Even successful writers who have an agent, entertainment attorney, or manager, create opportunities for themselves. If you do not subscribe to one of the trade papers, try your local library for copies or go in with a fellow scripter for a subscription. Both *Daily Variety* or *The Hollywood Reporter* occasionally offer free 30-day trial subscriptions.

Do not forget to scour the weekend entertainment sections of the larger metropolitan papers; they contain fodder for marketing prospects. Gossip columns, which often mention the name of a star's new production company, plus radio and television segments that focus on entertainment are also potential gold mines of current information, along with such magazines as *People* and *Premiere*.

Other marketing sources include the fore-mentioned *HCD* directories: primarily the three for *Producers*, *Distributors*, and *Agents & Managers*. Online sources include: Movie Bytes (*www.moviebytes.com*), Done Deal (*www.scriptsales.com*), Hollywood Lit Sales (*www.hollywoodlitsales.com*), and Internet Movie database (*www.us.imdb.com*).

Make notes or clip items and, if you are currently trying to market or sell your project, act upon them. If you are not quite at this point, file the items for further action in a separate marketing file (multi-compartment accordion files work well) until you are ready to make your move.

NETWORK

The most productive place to network is at a writing conference, film festival, or pitchfest. Here you will have opportunities to meet agents, producers, studio executives, writers, and other undiscovered scripters like yourself.

The importance of developing good networking skills cannot be stressed enough. Gathering and sharing information is a key component in succeeding and maintaining a career in the entertainment industry. The art of networking is so vital, the entire next chapter is devoted to the subject (see page 143).

If there is a local screenwriting group, consider joining. If there is not a group, think about starting one of your own. Or join an organization like the American Screenwriters Association, which has members worldwide who share information and critique one another's scripts while providing valuable advice and information on their association's Web site.

Become a volunteer at a nearby film festival or call your local film commission. Ask if you can volunteer at any events or spend a couple of hours each week as an intern there, or at a local television station or video production house. Often state film commissions will sponsor screenwriting competitions. If you are not yet ready to enter the competition, but would like to participate and gain a little insight into the screenwriting process, consider being a volunteer for the preliminary judging.

If a nearby college or university has a screenwriting course, think about taking the course, not only to gain additional knowledge and information, but to network with other course participants who might become valuable allies and supporters. These classes are also an ideal venue to find writers interested in joining a writing group.

If your local newspaper does not have a film critic and if you are an avid movie buff, take a leap of faith and call the paper and ask if they would be interested in hiring you. Of course, it is advisable to have a few sample critiques to demonstrate your writing style. If your local paper already has a film critic, she may be flattered if you ask if you can pick her brain about screenwriting.

All of the above are potential gardens of information to cultivate and harvest.

SEE MORE MOVIES

At the risk of sounding silly, when I advise seeing movies, I mean all kinds of movies. With the wide range of videos available and with so many movie channels on cable, there is no reason not to view at least one or two films a week. And while you may want to concentrate on great romantic classics because that is the genre of your current project, you should broaden your perspective.

Seeing all kinds of motion pictures means keeping an open mind and expanding your moviegoing knowledge by viewing "bad" movies and different genres, even those you do not particularly like. Writers can get a better understanding of what works and what does not work by watching films that are totally unfamiliar.

There is an art to watching films:

- If you are at a theater, sit as close to the middle of the theater as possible. Never sit in the first five rows (unless you are hard of hearing, have forgotten your glasses, or are in one of those tiny multi-screen theaters with only ten rows). I usually sit at least twelve rows from the front and five rows from the back because this allows me the most viewing pleasure and gives me a greater arena for audience observation.

- Before the lights dim, look around. What is the age range of the audience? Which age group makes up the greater percentage of those present? Is this audience composed mostly of males or females? What is the cultural, racial, and socio-economic makeup of the people there? This kind of information helps writers pinpoint the demographic appeal of a movie, one of the key elements when a production company or a studio decides whether to purchase your script. Some films appeal to a broader audience than others. Surprisingly, there are movies that, on the surface, seem to appeal to a narrower segment of moviegoers but end up "crossing over" and appealing to the general public. Some examples include *The Joy Luck Club*, *The Full Monty*, and *Shall We Dance?*

- As you watch the film, ask: What is this movie about? What is the hero's or heroine's main goal? Who or what serves as the protagonist's main challenge or opposition and why? Has anyone walked out yet? The first thirty minutes or so should provide the setup of the story and coincides with the first 30-35 pages of a script. If you are watching *Ghandi*, *Dances With Wolves*, or a Russian or an Indian film, you will need to allow slightly longer for the setup.

- By the end of the first hour, it is time to ask: Is the hero's or heroine's plan of action in place? Have there been enough complications and plot twists to keep the audience interested? Or are there so many subplots and story points that the film is becoming too plot-heavy? Conversely, is the story so simple and uneventful that the audience is quickly losing interest? This is the all-important mid-section of the story, where many a film (or script) can fall apart.

- Toward the end of the movie, you should notice if the audience is fully behind the hero's or heroine's attempts for success. Can you sense that people are rooting for the protagonist? In the more successful action films, the audience will sometimes talk back to the screen as they cheer the hero on to victory.

- Throughout the film, observe the following: Which scenes get the best response? Which scenes fall flat? What character(s) gets the best and the worst responses from the audience? Which lines make the audience react (i.e., laugh, cry, sigh, etc.)?

- As the audience files out, what are some of the comments you overhear? Does the audience stay for the credits (usually a sign that they did not want this movie experience to end)? Try to stay seated through the credits whenever possible. They may contain valuable information, such as where the film was shot, who provided those wonderful sets, what design house created those innovative titles, who the actor was whose two lines stole the scene in the first act, or what production company made the film. You never know when this information will prove useful.

- Once home, analyze the audience reaction using the following questions: Was the movie too long? Was it too short? Were there signs of restlessness from the audience and, if so, in which section of the story? Did you notice people constantly checking their watches? Did anyone walk out of the film? Why did the movie succeed or fail from the viewpoint of the story? Why did the movie succeed or fail in any other aspects, like direction, acting, etc.?

- Assess the "look" of the film by considering the locations, special effects, stunts, setting, and how much impact each of these elements played upon the overall movie. When evaluating scripts, story analysts will always consider whether the story justifies the cost of production. Obviously, the more commercial potential a film has, the more money the studio or the production company will be willing to spend on such high-ticket items as locations, effects, etc. It is also interesting to notice, if a film was set in a foreign locale or during a different historical period, did most of the story take place indoors (interiors, which can be shot on studio sets) or outdoors (exteriors, which require filming on location)?

- Assess other aspects of the film. Was there too much internal, thought-driven story (a difficult thing to communicate realistically on screen) and not enough external action, or vice versa? Were there scenes that required large numbers of extras? Did the stuntwork outshine the story? Consider the impact of such items as the musical score, costume design, and other production values, asking yourself if the final result lived up to the film's production values, that is, the amount spent on production? Remember that people want to value what they see and experience. Will they feel this film was worth the price of admission?

- Was this a high or low/soft concept film? In other words, was this a commercial film with an easy-to-understand focus and appeal (high-concept) or was it a more specialized, smaller film (low or soft concept) that might not appeal to a broader audience? Was the movie more plot-driven (action, adventure, and horror films usually fall into this category) or character-driven (dramas and love stories are prime examples)? Or was this that rare film that ably and successfully combined both plot and characterizations? (*A Beautiful Mind*, *The Shawshank Redemption*, and *The Fugitive* are good examples of this winning combination.)

- What was the marketing focus of the film? Did you see trailers for this movie? If so, did they successfully encourage you to see the film? Do you remember the trailers? What did they show? Look at the film's theater posters (one-sheets) and its newspaper and magazine ads for clues in how the audience was wooed. In many cases, moviegoers comment that the coming attraction for a film was far better than the actual film.

- Assess your gut reaction. Were you entertained by this movie? Would you recommend this film to your friends or family? If not, why? How could this film be improved from the viewpoint of story? Was there any part of the story that confused you? Did you understand each character's purpose and reason for being included in the story? Was the dialogue effective in helping to mold the growth and the personalities of the characters while moving the story forward?

GET INTO PEOPLE-WATCHING

Writers often mention that some of the best stories and characters come from simply observing life around them. Some of their favorite places to people-watch are crowded areas like airports, college campuses, parks, shopping malls, train or subway stations, amusement parks, parties, reunions, and restaurants. One writer tells me that some of his most colorful and interesting characters for his stories were "born" in Las Vegas, that is, he observed people who piqued his imagination and made him wonder: Who are they? Why are they in Las Vegas? Do they really want to be there? What do they do for a living? Do they have a family? What are they feeling at the moment (i.e., happy, lonely, confused, hopeful, unsure, etc.)?

Notice how people are dressed, along with their posture and their attitude. Are they self-assured and confident or the exact opposite? Do they have any unusual physical traits or mannerisms? Do they have any annoying habits or unique quirks? And, most of all, what do you think their story is up to this point in their lives?

Everyone has a history; it is fun to build a personality and a story around a person who catches your eye. One helpful hint: Do not be too obvious in your people-watching or your creative efforts might be misconstrued!

READ, READ, READ

In addition to your daily local newspaper (an absolute must), scan as many current affairs and specialty publications as you can. *Variety, The Hollywood Reporter, People,* and *Premiere* have already been mentioned, but consider looking at such publications as *Time, The American Medical Journal, Scientific Monthly, The Wall Street Journal, Prevention, Readers Digest,* and *Newsweek*. Read, not just for the entertainment segments of the magazine or the newspaper, but for that unexpected piece of information you might need for your project. Read to glean ideas and to provide background — maybe that article on battered women holds insights for the central character in your latest screenplay, or perhaps that new experimental drug could be the focus of your latest crime thriller.

When reading the trade papers, do not be tempted to read only the film and television reviews. The articles are chock full of information that can be valuable to you. As for the reviews, read beyond the first paragraph; see what you can learn from the particulars of the review: the critique of the storyline, plotting, characterization, dialogue, etc.

It is also important to read the reviews in major magazines, newspapers, and on Internet sites. (See page 128 for some sites.) All help to give you a wider perspective of what fare is in the theaters and how particular movies are perceived across the country. Note that the companies that distribute the films will often lift quotations from critics' reviews to help bolster a film's advertisements in newspapers, on billboards, and in television commercials. The quotes that writers should look for are those directly related to the screenplay, like "well-crafted story and characters" or "a spine-tingling thriller that will keep you guessing."

On a secondary level, note comments that reflect a critic's reasons for liking or disliking a film. For example, "Despite an intriguing story, the actor cannot seem to breathe much life into his role," or "Lush photography, coupled with brilliant costuming, adds to the visual appeal of this fascinating period piece."

As a matter of habit, most writers usually scan the weekly charts of the trade papers that feature the box office standings for the preceding week. These charts provide useful information about what kinds of films are popular, both initially and for the long run. When you read the charts, note the top ten films and pay particular attention to how many weeks each movie has been in release. If a film has been out longer than two weeks, compare its present ranking to the week before. Notice how many screens (theaters) carried the film. Higher concept, bigger-budgeted films like *Jurassic Park 3* or *The Lord of the Rings: The Fellowship of the Ring* are seen on more than 2,500 screens, while smaller, more character-driven specialty films like *An American Rhapsody* or *The Deep End* may be shown in only fifty theaters. An important number to note is the "per screen average" for each film, for that statistic really indicates how a movie is doing — no matter how wide or how limited its release. Consider the genre of each movie to determine what the public is going to see, but take heart that in two years, that genre may not be enjoying quite as much popularity.

The trade papers carry similar charts for international box office statistics. Note the popular genres and trends in the global marketplace, since a great deal of revenue comes from overseas sales. There are also charts for top video and DVD rentals and sales, which comprise a great deal of potential revenue for a feature film. The trades also include ratings charts for network TV offerings and syndicated TV shows.

Read the trades to keep up on the changes at studios, agencies, and production companies. Changes to look for include the promotion/ousting of key individuals whose jobs are to look at or buy screenplays — people such as vice presidents of production, directors of development, and executive story editors. A frequent expression used when a production head steps down is that he is "going indie prod," which means his attorney negotiated a deal allowing the ousted exec to become an independent producer (which could also mean a possible new venue to target for your next project).

Other changes to note in the trades might include a shift in the number of films being produced. Recently, a major studio announced plans to accelerate its feature film slate from twenty to twenty-five films a year. This acceleration was due to the studio's acquisition by a larger, financially healthy parent company. Acquisition also brings up another area of concern for writers: a change of ownership at a studio, large production company, or agency. Although these changes do not take place every day, they do seem to happen more frequently than in years past. Whenever a change in ownership occurs, it is sometimes best to wait until the new regime settles in before submitting material. With new ownership comes the distinct possibility of a change of production executives, with new decision makers or a shift of agents from one department or agency to another. It can also mean a shift in the types of films being produced.

Look for articles about the purchase of screenplays. A recent article said Studio X "nabbed the edgy sci-fi script for $500,000 against $800,000." The article further noted, "This move... illustrates the company's desire to diversify into producing more adult-focused projects as well as family fare." As you can see, the article gave the dollar amount spent, the genre of the script, as well as the added information that the studio was willing to take a chance on a more adult-focused project. Pay attention to any other information about screenplay sales, i.e., the key agents/agency involved, as well as any attachments (producer, director, actor). Sometimes the article will even give a *TV Guide*-type blurb on the script's premise.

The trade papers also have a weekly feature on films in development which states the genre of the film, the production company or the studio, as well as the appropriate addresses and phone numbers. Sometimes key personnel are also listed, giving you more names to put in your marketing file. If you are torn between writing a thriller or a romantic-comedy, it may help to look at the films in development. If there seems to be an overabundance of thrillers, you might want to start on your romantic-comedy idea first.

As mentioned earlier, valuable information can be found in gossip columns, especially in the trade papers. One column recently mentioned that a well-known action director credited his producer-wife with finding a high-tech thriller script. If you have a dynamite action screenplay, it might be worth the time to find out the name of the wife's production company and target her on your "A" list of producers. Chances are in your favor that if she wants to produce your project, she may be able to get her "hot" director husband to lens your movie.

ASK QUESTIONS

Questions should be part of your networking skills. When you make a new acquaintance, ask about his work. Ask about his travels, family, and interests. You would be surprised how easy it is to find someone who knows someone else who is knowledgeable and willing to discuss an area of expertise. Most people are flattered when a writer asks for an expert opinion, especially when they know what they say might be used in a script.

When friends and acquaintances cannot pave the way to an appropriate expert, experienced writers often "let their fingers do the walking" and make cold calls to the local American Cancer Society, the neighborhood branch of the public library, or the community-relations office of the city police department. And if you are writing in the middle of the night and cannot call anyone for information, the Internet is an excellent and inexpensive source to find out basic information on just about any disease, organization, country, language, or subject you can possibly imagine.

STRIVE TO BE PROFESSIONAL

One observation about many emerging screenwriters is that they do not always present themselves in a professional way. As a writer, you will always have some area you can work on to achieve a more polished, professional presence. Perhaps you need to develop better phone skills or are having problems with writing your query letters. Maybe it is time to take a seminar on sales techniques to gain more insight on how to sell yourself and your work without going overboard.

One working writer told me that the best workshop she took was one on marketing. She learned how to ask questions that would encourage others to be more open about sharing information. She learned which questions would elicit more than a "yes" or a "no." And after taking the marketing class, she was more observant about doing the proper research, whether it was on the location of her new project, creating a new character, or narrowing down the list of production companies that would be best to approach regarding her just-finished script.

Being professional also means not taking rejection personally. It means being open to suggestions and criticisms as long as they are constructive. It means taking pride in yourself, but knowing when not to let your pride stand in the way of conducting yourself professionally.

CHAPTER 11

NETWORKING — NAVIGATING YOUR WAY THROUGH THE INDUSTRY MAZE

When I was an exec at Disney, my assistant buzzed me on the intercom. Someone named David was on the phone, insisting he'd met me recently. Thinking that it might have been a person I had spoken to at an industry party, I took the call. David turned out to be a "writer" with a script he wanted to submit. When I asked him where we'd met, he hemmed and hawed before finally confessing he'd sold me a pair of shoes a few days ago. I asked him how he got my number and he reminded me that he had asked for my place of employment, as was the store's policy whenever a purchase was made by check. He finally admitted it wasn't store policy, but he'd spotted a couple of scripts in my tote bag and wanted to find out where I worked, hopeful that selling me a pair of shoes was all the networking he needed to do to get his big break...WRONG!

One of the toughest tasks for a writer is the art of networking. Let's face it, writers are used to being locked in a dark, dingy garret, far away from the normal light-filled world, alone with no one else but their faithful dog and their computer. It is not part of a writer's natural instinct to seek out and share information or ask for favors from the outside world.

Unfortunately, more than any other kind of writer, a screenwriter will find his career path can fail if the art of networking is not among his arsenal of talents. The entertainment industry and the rise of anyone participating in the Biz is usually in direct proportion to who you know, what you know, and what you do with those contacts and knowledge.

WHAT IS NETWORKING?

In short, **networking** is the fine art of meeting, greeting, and assimilating with others who usually share a common interest — in this case, writing for the television, film, and entertainment industries.

WHO NETWORKS?

Nearly every person who has a modicum of success in the entertainment industry finds that networking is a vital and integral part of her life — from studio execs to agents, from producers to writers, from assistants to those who would like to be part of this crazy business. Any serious screenwriter who would like her latest script to be read for representation by an agent or for consideration as a project by a production company should look upon networking as a natural off-shoot of her writing talent.

WHY IS NETWORKING SO IMPORTANT?

Networking, along with talent (be it acting, directing, writing, deal-making, producing, etc.), is the lifeblood of the entertainment industry. Cultivating relationships can lead to unexpected opportunities. Networking, when properly done, can be informative, productive, and often lead to friendship as well as some helpful door-opening. WARNING: Successful networking is based upon mutual respect; one-sided, self-serving relationships are strongly discouraged.

PREPARATION
If you are planning to attend a conference, pitchfest, or film festival, here are some pre-event pointers to keep in mind:

- Read the conference brochure or program thoroughly, paying careful attention to the faculty members or the special guests who will be attending. Most brochures or programs include a brief biographical sketch. If bios are not included, do not be afraid to call the organization that is putting on the event to ask for brief credentials on the speakers.

- Select two or three speakers or guests whose credentials are in line with your needs and interests. In other words, if you have just completed a comedy about a family that is lost in space, it would be more productive to focus on meeting the producer or the studio exec who has worked on a family feature, rather than the independent filmmaker who specializes in low-budget horror films. Note that I have suggested keying in on two or three guests. While some overzealous writers may want to meet and greet every single faculty member, it is unwise to spend every minute of the conference or festival networking, and lose out on gathering valuable information from the workshops.

- If you are unfamiliar with someone's credits, do some research. *The Hollywood Creative Directories, Halliwell's Guide to Movies,* and *The Internet Movie Database* are very helpful resources to use, especially if you want to find out about the unfamiliar film that a producer worked on. Doing a search online can usually deliver film reviews or additional information about the production company, studio, or agency. Some resourceful writers have found it helpful to view the speakers' past work on video, providing additional topics of conversation when networking with them or other attendees.

- Read the trade papers for up-to-the-minute information. Become familiar with common terms used in the entertainment industry. Be sure to scan the weekly film and television production sections of the trades, noting which companies or studios are doing family-oriented projects and might be future production houses to target when you complete your new kid's adventure film. Take careful note of projects that mention faculty members. (Producers, writers, etc., are complimented when someone mentions their latest work.)

- Carefully plan your schedule to include those workshops, panels, screenings, and sessions which will be most appropriate and in line with your interests. Accept the fact that you will never be everywhere at once. Just a warning: Workshop-hopping can be hazardous. Listening to half of a session will probably only give you half the picture and may end up more confusing than enlightening. Jot down some questions which pertain to the workshops or the panels you have selected. Hopefully, the speaker or panelists will be able to address those questions during the session. If the question was thought-provoking, it may also be a point of discussion, should you happen to see that speaker later during the event.

- If the conference allows, take advantage of scheduling a consultation with one or more of the faculty or workshop speakers. Keep in mind, however, that there are a limited number of both consultations and faculty members. Try to be flexible by giving conference organizers three or four choices of faculty members. Also, be aware that speakers may only be available at certain time periods, which might mean missing part of another session. Most attendees will agree that if given a choice between attending a workshop and having a 10-minute consultation, the consultation would be the best bet. Most importantly, many conferences will assign consultations based on early registration, that is, whichever attendees register first will most likely get their preferred choice of a prized consultation.

WHILE ATTENDING THE EVENT
- If you were unable to obtain a consultation with a speaker, be sure to check with the conference staff for possible cancellations. Often, you will be put on a waiting list.

- Remember that networking can be done throughout the conference or the festival. Many conferences set aside specific times which are particularly geared for interaction between special guests and event attendees. However, some networking can be done between workshops and during meals, as long as common courtesy is shown (i.e., if a speaker is seated at your table during lunch, please allow her to finish her lunch before bombarding her with

147

questions). And as always, ask one question at a time, allowing other participants to speak with her as well.

- If a speaker or a panelist has not covered a specific area or if you are unclear about a point he has addressed, do not be shy about raising your hand and asking questions or for further clarification. All questions should be asked in a courteous and non-combative manner. One writer, eager to prove a point and hopefully get himself noticed, did so in a brash and aggressive manner, which did not endear him to the panelists or the members of the audience. When he later ran into the speaker at the event party, the speaker was only coolly polite. The writer quickly realized his brashness was a mistake.

ADDITIONAL NETWORKING HINTS

- Remember to network with other attendees. Some writers are so busy pursuing faculty members that they overlook the more lasting value of networking with other writers and conference attendees. Most events supply badges or nametags with the attendees' names and sometimes their hometowns. If you have been looking for a screenwriting critique group, it would be very beneficial to network with others who live in your general area. If you happen to strike up a friendship with another writer, perhaps you could pool your notes. If you have a consultation with a speaker or have a scheduling conflict, doing a little shared networking could produce an offer to make a copy of an audiotape or notes on the missed session. Several writers have found writing partners by networking at an event.

• Learn to ask questions that require more than just a simple "yes" or "no" answer. As successful businesspersons in marketing and sales will tell you, it is important to master the art of asking open-ended questions (i.e., "What do you think about...," "How would you feel if...," etc.). Asking open-ended questions can result in a more thorough answer and also gives others the impression that you are genuinely interested in their advice, comments, and/or opinions.

• During a workshop, panel, or question and answer session, it is advisable to confine your questions to the specific area covered (i.e., if the workshop is about TV sitcoms, it would be preferable not to ask about dramatic structure). In general, attendees might want to raise specific questions regarding their personal projects during a consultation with a faculty member rather than during a workshop. If, however, a producer has mentioned he has a particular interest in an arena which coincides with your project, you can always mention it after the Q & A session if the opportunity presents itself. There are no guarantees that the producer, exec, or agent will ask to see your script, but it is a way of relaying the information. If the producer is amenable, he may contact you during the conference. If you are shy or if there is not enough time to get to you before the session ends, it is perfectly acceptable to talk with the speaker or the panelist between workshops or sessions or during a networking opportunity, as long as the speaker is not hurrying off to another scheduled commitment.

• If you are fortunate enough to have a consultation with a faculty member, be fully prepared with a few key questions. Starting out a consultation by handing an agent your script and asking him to represent you is not the suggested way to network. Instead, give the agent a little background on yourself. If you have published works in other areas of writing, mention that. If you have more than one script (always "music" to an agent's ears), give a logline on each to see if any piques his interest, remembering that agents want writers who are in for the long haul and have screenplays they can sell. If your consultation is with a producer or a studio exec, they are more likely to be impressed if you ask about their future development slate or if their projects must meet specific budgetary demands. Keep in mind that most studio execs are unable to accept submissions unless they come from a producer, an agent, or an entertainment attorney. Consultations with studio execs and producers can give writers valuable information about the types of projects studios are looking for or what actors and directors have production deals with them. Whether the faculty member is an agent, producer, exec, writer, or consultant, attendees can always find out more about the industry marketplace and any discernable turn-ons or turn-offs.

• Remember that the most successful networking is when both parties receive shared benefits. Like friendships and marriages, the best networking relationships survive when there is give and take on both sides, coupled with a healthy and genuine dose of mutual respect.

- As Forrest Gump would say, "My mama always told me to say 'please' and 'thank you.'" If a fellow attendee, speaker, or workshop leader was especially helpful or made a positive impression on you — either during his workshop, consultation, or at a networking event — you may want to send a brief follow-up note of thanks. This approach is another way to extend your networking once the conference or the event has concluded. If you did not receive a business card, you can always address your thank-you note to the organization that sponsored the event and they will pass it on.

- Post-conference, continue to keep in touch with other conference attendees who were helpful and shared similar writing and life philosophies. This practice greatly increases the opportunities for mutual benefit if one of you should become successful. With the Internet, there is absolutely no reason why you cannot stay in touch! As one writer mentioned to me, "It's great to have an understanding shoulder to cry on when you get writer's block."

- Be generous to others in the hopes that what goes around, comes around. Do not be shy about letting others know of your success. It provides hope and encouragement to all. Greet and speak to others using direct eye contact and always remember that a friendly smile goes a long way.

Networking Faux Pas

Here are some actual examples of what not to do where networking is concerned:

CROSSING THE LINE

Not long ago, I received a call from an agent who had participated on a panel with me. He started out the conversation: "So you think this writer has potential, huh? She said she was one of your students and was sending me her screenplay at your suggestion." Much as I tried, I couldn't recall this writer (let's call her Dawn). I had to set the record straight.

While Dawn may have taken one of my classes or workshops, I had not personally recommended her to this agent or any other agent. This overzealous writer, whose effort may sound creative to some, had crossed the line and, in doing so, may have done herself more harm than good.

It is important to understand that the entertainment industry is built on networking relationships and personal favors. While some writers may get away with half-truths and finger-crossing, most will do better by not starting off on the wrong side of the line. Clearly Dawn had not expected the agent to call me.

I wish this had been a one-time occurrence, but similar scenarios occur at least three or four times a year. Unfortunately, this kind of thing happens to many of my colleagues in the industry as well.

Here's an example of a better alternative for Dawn:

Dawn should schedule a 10-minute consultation with the agent at the conference. During the consultation, she should ask the agent about the marketplace. What genres are selling? Which studios/production companies are looking for strong, character-driven dramas (or whatever is the focus of Dawn's latest project)? She should query the agent about how large the agency is and what kind of writing talent its agents are looking for (i.e., sitcom writers, feature writers, animation writers, etc.).

Armed with information she has gathered from the trade papers, Dawn could then discuss her latest work which might be appropriate for a particular star (who just happens to be a client of this agency).

Perhaps at a networking session during the event, Dawn could reconnect with the agent and mention other projects she is working on that might tie in with information brought up during other sessions or workshops. Her approach would show initiative and lets the agent know that she is not only productive but takes her writing seriously.

THE ONE-SIDED OPPORTUNIST

One overly-eager writer (we'll call him Tom) asked it he could sit in on a writers group session to see if he would fit in. During the session, he spoke with an up-and-coming writer whose screenplay had just been optioned by a noted producer. Tom asked the writer if she would introduce him to this producer. The writer said she would be happy to "when the time was right."

Tom promptly sent his script to the producer, using the writer's name as his entry. Obviously, he felt the time was right *now*. You can imagine the writer's embarrassment when the producer called several weeks later to say that Tom's work was mediocre and totally inappropriate for his company. Tom, by the way, only attended that one meeting of the writers group and never returned, having gotten what he thought he came for: a possible key contact. However, he left a potential colleague with egg on her face; she will probably be unwilling to help him out again.

Here's how Tom could have approached things in a more productive and professional way:

Tom sits in on the writers group and spends the first half of the meeting listening carefully, assessing personalities, and discovering where the various members are in their writing (absolute beginner, more experienced writer with work optioned, someone with sample scripts who wants an agent, etc.). Tom also gauges his comfort level within the group.

During a break, Tom chats with at least two members. Then, if he is comfortable, he begins participating actively in the rest of the session, but only if he has constructive comments to make. This approach allows the rest of the group to get to know him. If his contributions are helpful and positive, it is likely he will fit in.

Once invited to join, Tom attends the writers group for a few months, getting to know the members and allowing them to get to know him as well. When he learns that certain members have agents or have had the good fortune to get material read or optioned, he asks them for advice on how he might achieve similar results.

With this approach, members of the group will most likely want to help Tom. They will probably want to read his work before they refer him to a producer or an agent. This is standard procedure whenever a writer asks anyone in the industry (be it exec, producer, agent, etc.) for a favor or a referral. The person extending the favor has to know and believe in your work because her reputation is on the line with every recommendation.

SOME REAL-LIFE RESULTS
In their desperation to be recognized and to achieve their goals,

154

over-zealous writers like Dawn and Tom failed to recognize and acknowledge the following:

- The film and television industry is a relatively small community where no one is more than one person away from knowing someone else.

- The industry thrives on networking. The relationships among agents, producers, directors, actors, writers, consultants, and executives are not be to taken lightly.

- Because this community is so very close-knit, a considerable amount of news is shared and traded — including information, gossip, and occasionally stories like the two that have been shared above.

- It is often said that a person in this industry is only as good as his or her last movie, last role, last script, or last faux pas!

MAKING THE MOST OF FAVORS

As is the case in any line of work, those with the power to hire prefer one quality person to ten mediocre ones. This opinion is especially true in the entertainment industry. Therefore, recommendations and favors are to be taken seriously and are not given out to everyone.

If you are fortunate enough to be given a true opportunity, think of it as the only favor this person may ever grant you. Value what you have been given (no matter what the outcome) and be certain that the work you submit is at its best and will not embarrass you or the person recommending you. And, most of all, remember that sharing your knowledge and opportunities with others is part of the process.

CHAPTER 12

YOU ARE NOT ALONE — GROUP THERAPY FOR WRITERS AKA GETTING THE MOST OUT OF WRITING CONFERENCES AND WRITERS GROUPS

One of the best ways to take away the self-doubt that most writers put upon themselves from time to time is to meet other writers. "But where?" you ask. Why not attend a writing conference where you can meet other writers and also make valuable industry contacts, sharpen your creative skills, and expand your education as a writer? Or why not consider joining or starting a writers group in your area or online?

In the past several years, more conferences have featured screenwriting as the major or sole focus of their event. From Seattle to Michigan, from Austin to Hawaii, from Vancouver to Santa Fe, universities, film commissions, and large networks of writers are sponsoring screenwriting days, pitchfests, and weekend conferences. While admission to these events can be anywhere from free to several hundred dollars, they can be a productive and beneficial way for screenwriters to stay connected.

GETTING READY
If you have made the decision to attend one of these events, prepare yourself mentally. While it is a good idea to establish goals for

yourself, be realistic. Know in advance that there are no guaranteed rules for breaking into screenwriting. "Overnight successes" are most assuredly the exception rather than the rule.

At conferences, speakers, panelists, and consultants each offer their own set of guidelines, methods, or advice that have worked for them. As most of us should be wise enough to know, what works for one person will not necessarily work for all. However, advice and information should always be greeted with an open mind and respect for the person who is sharing his knowledge with you and the other writers in attendance.

Here is some preparation you can do in advance:

- Read the conference brochure carefully and decide your schedule. If the conference offers first-come, first-served appointments with faculty members, be sure to sign up early to avoid disappointment.

- Review the brochure and select the workshops and the panels that are appropriate for your level of experience. Plan to attend classes that will sharpen your skills and/or benefit your particular area of interest (or weakness), such as character development, structure, television/cable movies, sitcoms, etc. If two interesting workshops are scheduled at the same time, make a note to look for someone you can share notes with — someone who will attend one session while you attend the other.

- If you have special needs (such as dietary requirements for meals, a handicapped-accessible room, etc.), you will want to read the conference material carefully to see if these needs are addressed. If you do not see the information you need, do not be shy about calling the conference organizers to ask if these requests can be handled in advance.

- Make a checklist of materials to bring to the conference: note pads, plenty of writing instruments, business cards (if you have them), tape recorder, tapes, and batteries (always check in advance with conference personnel or speakers to find out if taping is allowed). If you are feeling particularly optimistic, you might want to bring along a copy or two of your treatment or your script.

- If you arrive early, check out the areas where your workshops will be held. Be sure to note where conference rooms are located in relation to one another and to the registration desk, dining area, and rest rooms.

- During registration, ask conference staff members if there are any last-minute changes not listed on the program (such as cancelled workshops, substitute speakers, room changes, etc.). If applicable, you may want to adjust your own schedule accordingly.

ATTENDING SESSIONS

During a workshop, make it a point to sit as close to the front of the room as you can — especially if you plan to tape the session and take accurate notes. Depending on the size of the room, the speaker may not use a microphone. If you are sitting at the back, you may spend a great deal of effort straining to hear the speaker; if you are trying to tape the session, your recorder will be less than effective.

Many regular workshop leaders enjoy communicating with the audience, an effort that is much harder to achieve if the audience is scattered all over the room. If you know in advance that you may have to leave a session early (say, for a one-on-one meeting), select a seat next to the aisle and closer to the door.

Of course, you will want to comply with all conference guidelines or rules. These are usually stated in the conference program or posted at the registration desk or mentioned at the start of the event. They often include wearing nametags or badges at all times, not smoking or eating in the conference rooms, or not taping a session without asking a speaker's permission. If a speaker declines your request to tape a session, it might be due to one of two possibilities: The speaker may work for a large company or corporation which will not allow her to be taped, or the speaker may be an author whose audio and visual rights are under contract to the publisher.

Be aware that with few exceptions, all sessions must begin and end on time to prevent a domino effect that could throw the entire day's conference schedule off.

WORKSHOP COURTESY
Here are some suggestions to help you get the most out of each workshop that you attend:

- Feel free to ask questions, especially during the question-and-answer period at the end of a workshop. If you do not understand a particular point made by the speaker, raise your hand and ask for further explanation. Few presenters mind valid interruptions, and chances are there may be someone else in the room who needs clarification.

- Try not to monopolize a speaker's time by asking more than one question, especially if there are others who have their hands raised. Also, address speakers and fellow participants in a positive manner, even if your thoughts and comments are not in line with theirs.

- During seminars, be sure to state your questions succinctly and clearly so everyone can hear. Prepare specific questions in advance for each of the workshops you will be attending. If your question is not answered during the speaker's formal presentation, take advantage of the question-and-answer session that usually follows.

- When a workshop comes to a close, refrain from crowding the speaker when he is leaving the stage/podium area. Keep in mind that the room usually needs to be cleared and readied for the next workshop. Also, inadvertently holding a speaker "at bay" makes it difficult for him to stay on schedule.

- Most workshops provide adequate time to ask questions at the end of a session. If, for some reason, you were unable to ask yours, wait until the speaker has left the classroom before you ask. If the speaker does not have to rush off to another commitment, he should be happy to answer your query. In return, do not try to turn the answer into a personal consultation.

NETWORKING COURTESY

Probably one of the highlights of many of the writing conferences is the networking events which enable faculty members and speakers to mingle with the attendees. In addition to any one-on-one appointments you are fortunate enough to obtain, networking get-togethers are your golden opportunity to make contacts and gather information.

- If you want to ask a question during such an event, make a good impression by politely waiting your turn and keeping your question brief and to the point. Remember that other participants are eagerly awaiting their turns, too.

- While it is great to be assertive, no one appreciates people who ungraciously monopolize a speaker's time, rudely interrupt others, or go overboard by not respecting a speaker's privacy. I once witnessed a writer at a conference who was so desperate to have her script read that she followed an agent into the women's rest room and pushed the script under the stall door. Needless to say, the agent firmly rejected this act, and the writer was told by conference personnel to keep a respectful distance from the agent or she would be asked to leave.

- If you are lucky enough to obtain a one-on-one appointment with a speaker, plan your agenda in advance. Determine three to five questions you want to ask, keeping in mind that most appointments last a mere ten minutes. If you opt to pitch your project during a one-on-one, practice in advance — again, keeping a careful eye on the clock. Allow five minutes for your pitch and five minutes for feedback from the speaker.

- Because of time restrictions, it is unwise to ask a speaker to read a few scenes or a synopsis of your work and to make comments. Also, be aware that many agents, executives, and producers cannot accept your screenplay at a conference — mostly for legal reasons, but also for logistical ones (few speakers have enough room in their suitcases to lug home forty scripts).

- Carefully consider which key presenters you would like to meet during the networking events. If there is a producer who specializes in family entertainment and you have a "boy and his dog" project, you would be wise to put this speaker at the top of your networking list. If your latest comedy is perfect for Adam Sandler, make it a point to speak with the development exec whose studio has a deal with the comedian.

ADDITIONAL ADVICE

The following are additional suggestions and advice from veterans of writers conferences:

- If you are unable to obtain an appointment with a particular speaker, try asking a conference staff member to put you on a waiting list in case of a cancellation. Then be sure that staff members know where you will be in case they need to reach you. Conversely, if you are unable to keep an appointment, let conference personnel know as soon as possible so they can give someone else the opportunity to meet and query the speaker.

- Type-A personalities will probably ignore this advice, but consider making time to relax during a conference. These events provide so much information packed into such a brief span of time that a break should be considered a mandatory part of your schedule. You might take a short walk between sessions or go to your room for a brief nap. If your schedule offers absolutely no time for breaks during the day, be sure to allow plenty of time to rest at the end of each evening. You might want to take fifteen minutes before bed to quietly evaluate what you have absorbed.

- It is an unfortunate fact that the roster of speakers at conferences is subject to change. Even though it is the goal of conference organizers to make every effort to maintain workshops and speakers as originally planned, there are times when changes are necessary and unavoidable. Instead of letting such changes throw you off course, re-evaluate your goals and seek out other opportunities and contacts.

- If there is a situation that deserves immediate action (such as not enough handouts, not enough seats, etc.), seek out a staff member to rectify the circumstances.

- Most conferences provide evaluation forms that give you a forum for your suggestions or complaints. If your experience was a positive one, you may want to introduce yourself to the conference director or a staff member to express your praise in person. In any case, do take the time to express your thoughts on the evaluation form. Let conference leaders know which events and/or faculty members were outstanding. Conversely, if you were disappointed with a workshop, explain why the session did not meet your expectations. These commentaries are valuable tools for planning future conferences; your feedback may ensure that your needs and those of the others attending will be met.

- In addition to networking with faculty members, do not forget to network with the other writers attending. Writing is such a solitary art, many find it extremely beneficial to share their experiences with others who are also waiting for the "big break." Participants at past conferences have ended up forming critique groups, sharing and comparing workshop notes, and have benefited from an exchange of knowledge by pooling information.

GROUP THERAPY

As stated earlier, a growing phenomenon among writers (novelists and non-fiction scribes, as well as screenwriters) is joining a writers or critique group. Although writing, on the surface, seems to be primarily a solo effort, you will find that what happens during the writing, as well as after you write "FADE OUT," is actually a collaborative effort. Screenwriters, especially those starting out, can benefit greatly from joining a writers group.

DISCOVERING SOME OF THE BENEFITS

One of the toughest issues a new writer faces is staying focused on the work at hand. When you only have *you* to answer to, it is sometimes tempting to go off track. Belonging to a group that shares a common desire to put pen to paper (or computer to laser or inkjet) goes a very long way toward keeping you committed, disciplined, and focused keenly on your writing.

Another obvious benefit of belonging to a group is the ability to share information, problems, and possible solutions. You would be surprised how many areas of concern all writers share. There is the ole' nemesis, writer's block, as well as self-doubt, lack of motivation, and creating a more exciting ending for Act II — to name a few.

In addition to offering suggestions to enhance a group member's work, those writers who band together also give emotional support, encouragement, and, as one writer told me, have even given members a job during the lean and discouraging times that often occur.

Many successful writers have benefited from participating in a writers group early in their careers.

Another benefit can be financial in nature. Imagine how much money can be saved if a group of people chip in to buy, circulate, and share materials such as copies of notable screenplays, reference materials, a subscription to a trade paper, etc. A subscription to *Variety* or *The Hollywood Reporter* can set you back a few hundred dollars a year. Imagine dividing that cost by four or five people. *The Hollywood Creative Directory's Producers* is about $55 an issue. But for $11 each, five people can share the cost.

One of a group's greatest benefits, however, is the power of net-working. It is not uncommon for a successful member to help another talented writer by introducing his or her work to an agent, producer, or executive. Such help is encouraged because the entertainment industry is fickle, and no one knows when your time in the spotlight may shift and you will need the support of others. Also, the genuine friendship and respect that develops among writers is probably one of the best perks of all.

FINDING OR STARTING YOUR OWN GROUP
First of all, it is advisable for members of a writers group to be "geographically desirable" if possible. However, with the advent of the Internet, there are dozens of writing and critique groups that have been in operation for several years online — their members' geographical locations are not important. Also, it is fairly easy to find chat rooms for screenwriters and form groups from there.

If you prefer meeting your group in person (the preference of many writers), it can be as easy as attending a writers conference (such as *Selling to Hollywood*) and talking to other attendees. As

mentioned earlier, many of the conferences encourage such networking by adding the hometown under the participant's name on
his badge. One *Selling to Hollywood* veteran told me that he saw a
plea on the message board of the conference which read: "Am I
the only person in the Lansing, Michigan area who is writing
screenplays?", followed by the person's name. By the end of the
conference, there were four people who lived within an hour's
drive who had contacted him. A writers' group was formed
instantly .

If you are taking a writing or a film class at a local university or
college, consider bringing up the idea of a writing or critique
group in your class. Other possibilities might include posting
inquiries at bookstores or gathering information from little theater
groups, drama or literature classes, film societies, film festival
offices, state or city film commissions, or friends and family who
may have acquaintances or neighbors who have expressed an
interest in screenwriting.

It is helpful, but not mandatory, to have members at relatively
the same stage of development or writing knowledge. It is also
advisable to limit the number of participants so everyone will get
the opportunity to have his or her work presented and critiqued
on a regular basis. If a large number of writers wish to join,
division by writing experience is a possible solution: for example,
beginners, those with a screenplay already started, those with at
least one script completed, etc.

Set up a mutually agreeable date and time for your meetings.
Groups can meet bimonthly, once a month, or even once a quarter.
Make sure your meeting place has comfortable seating and will be
relatively free of disturbances. Meeting at a restaurant is fine if
the management does not mind and the restaurant has a small

room that is separate from the main dining areas and is relatively quiet. Meeting in someone's home is ideal if there is room for all members. Libraries, local colleges and universities, and occasionally banks will have "community rooms" that are open to community groups.

ESTABLISHING GUIDELINES

Now that your group has agreed where and how often to meet, you should next decide to develop a mutual agenda. Some groups use the meetings exclusively for critiquing, while others make room for sharing writing-related information they have come across since the last meeting. Some groups focus on the work of one or two members per meeting, especially if the group has more than five or six members.

The group needs to agree that each member will write a certain number of pages or scenes before the next time they meet. At each meeting, make sure there are enough copies of each member's work for each person present. Decide if the work will be sent to members in advance of the meeting (either by snail mail, e-mail, or fax) or if time will be set aside for reading during the meeting.

Some of the more successful writers groups assign a group leader to remind others of meetings and to keep the discussion on track. Rotate this position periodically to avoid overburdening any one particular member.

When you have something to contribute, you must also be fully prepared to participate. Always be honest in your praise and constructive in your criticism. When commenting, try to put yourself in the recipient's shoes; unnecessarily harsh criticisms, petty remarks, and personal judgments have no place in these discussions. Be open-minded to the opinions and the suggestions of others, and they will usually show you the same well-deserved respect.

Always be on time. Everyone's time is valuable. And be sure that your work is ready. Are there enough copies? Is your work legible and in proper form? Be sure to "pass the spotlight" on to others by not taking more than your share of the time allotted for each person's work.

Consider setting aside some time at the end of each meeting for members to share good news, writing-related or otherwise. If the group is especially close, you can share bad news as well. One writer told me that if it were not for her passion for writing and the pep talks given to her by members of her group, she may not have made it through her divorce. But never lose sight of the purpose of the group: to support and encourage one another's writing efforts. Try to keep the "green-eyed monster" under control. If someone gets an option or an agent, be gracious and celebrate the success — you never know when that member might help you to make a valuable connection.

Finally, it is crucial that all members remember the cardinal rule of all writers groups: Keep all materials and discussions confidential. No ifs, ands, or buts on this guideline!

KNOWING WHEN TO LEAVE

While some relationships survive through the worst of storms, there may come a time when you feel a need to leave your writers group. Perhaps the group has lost its focus or has veered from its original goal of supporting members' writing ambitions. Or maybe an unforeseen personal problem in your life must take precedence over your writing. Change is understandable. If you feel you are falling behind or if you cannot carry through on your responsibilities to the other members of the group, do not be afraid to leave the group or ask if you can take a temporary break.

If you suddenly find Lady Fortune smiling down on you and you have more writing assignments than you can handle, you will likely be too busy to stay in a writers group. Yet one of the greatest benefits of such a group is the friendships that can form through the years. I know of one group of writers who are all doing well — two of them are TV staff writers, one is a highly successful writer/director, and two have had some produced work — yet they continue to meet each month to play poker and kick around story ideas between antes.

CHAPTER 13

A WORD TO THE WISE — AGENTS, LAWYERS, CONSULTANTS, AND OTHER POSSIBLE DISASTERS

Are you aware that many writers have been known to zealously protect their scripts by putting a copy in the freezer in case of a fire? Unfortunately, one writer's neighborhood suffered a twenty-hour power outage. It wasn't until a day later that she discovered her beloved script, which was now a soggy disaster.

Once you have written a script, you are likely to be looking for someone who can help you take your work to market. But whom should you turn to? An agent? An entertainment attorney? A manager? A script consultant? How best can you protect your work?

WHAT IS AN AGENT?
Next to your own writing talent, a good agent can be a writer's greatest asset. An **agent** represents you by presenting your work

to a variety of entertainment industry entities, such as studios, production companies, networks, and cable companies.

WHAT CAN AN AGENT DO FOR ME?

Good agents can save you a lot of precious time, energy, and expense by doing most of the marketing you would have to do if you were not represented. They can open doors with ease if they have made solid contacts at major production venues. They keep their contacts current with frequent phone calls, lunches, and/or visits to query about the types of projects being sought and to ask about writing assignments that need to be filled.

When you are stuck on a project, a good agent can serve as a sounding board — offering advice, encouragement, and constructive criticism. Good agents can do research on your behalf when it comes time for negotiations. They know when to take the initiative to push ahead, but above all, they know never to walk away from a fair deal.

DO I NEED AN AGENT?

If you live out of the Southern California area and do not have the finances to afford monthly phone, postage, and courier bills, nor the time to spend writing and marketing yourself, then you would be better off with an agent.

Having an agent in the Los Angeles area (or at least an agent who is a signatory to the Writers Guild of America) guarantees that you will be represented by someone who is fully cognizant of the professional guidelines and the courtesies that exist in the entertainment industry. In other words, a good agent knows how to do business in the entertainment community. This skill is especially important if you, the agent's client, live outside the greater Los Angeles area.

Sheer economics is also a major ongoing factor to consider. Frequent phone calls, faxing of writing credits, messenger charges to deliver writing samples, and business lunches and dinners are expensive but accepted ways for agents to establish solid relationships with each of their contacts. Good agents have dozens, sometimes hundreds, of professional contacts at different venues. Keeping up on the needs of these contacts while matching those needs with the talents and the abilities of their represented writers is not always an easy task.

Yes, there are a few writers who do not have agents and manage to do well. But most of them had an agent to get them started on the road to a successful career. Also, if further queried, many of those un-agented writers would have to admit that instead of an agent, they have high-powered entertainment attorneys or business managers to represent them, all of whom demand hefty annual retainers, plus any incurred legal costs.

HOW MUCH DOES AN AGENT GET?
Agents who are signatories to the Writers Guild of America get the same fee: 10 percent of a writer's gross fee. It cannot be stressed enough: Do not retain an agent who is not WGA-affiliated, and never give any money up front to an agent, even if the agent claims to be WGA-affiliated.

WHY SHOULD THE AGENT BE WGA-AFFILIATED?
Unfortunately, there are dozens of horror stories I have heard — mostly from out-of-area writers who were conned out of hundreds, sometimes thousands, of dollars by so-called "agents" who were not WGA-approved. If you are not sure whether an agent is a WGA signatory, simply contact the Writers Guild of America west — at (323)951-4000 (phone) or (323)782-4800 (fax) or *www.wga.org* — and ask for a list of agents who are signatories.

How Do I Get an Agent?
This is probably the question I'm most frequently asked.

The very best way to get an agent is if you have a connection who can refer you. A connection can mean a friend, relative, business associate, or casual acquaintance. A writer I know got her script to an agent because her apartment manager happened to mention that he played tennis with one. She cooked a spaghetti dinner for the apartment manager, who gave the script to his tennis partner, who eventually became the writer's first agent.

If you do not have a connection for a referral, the best place to start is by logging on to the WGA Web site and clicking onto the section regarding agents. There will be instructions on how to request the Guild's approved agency list. Although the numbers are small, some agencies (even some that say they are not accepting submissions) will accept material from new writers. If you send a query to one of these agencies, remember to enclose a SASE. It is helpful to begin working on your next script while you wait for a response. It may takes weeks (yes, even months) for agents to work their way through the ever-growing piles of correspondence sent to them.

In your query letter, keep things brief and to the point. The letter should never be more than a page long. You should include your project's title and a one- or two-sentence logline. If you are a published writer, you can briefly mention that. If you have more than one script, do not be afraid to say, "I have two completed comedy scripts and am working on my third." This statement indicates that you are not a one-script wonder and that you are interested in a full-time career as a screenwriter.

One agent told me her interest was piqued when an emerging screenwriter sent her a query letter in which he mentioned that he was a former FBI agent who had to quit the Bureau because of a work-related injury. Since his logline stated that the hero of his script is an FBI agent who uncovers a covert espionage squad within the government, the literary agent was immediately intrigued and asked to see the script.

WHAT DO I DO IF I DO NOT GET A POSITIVE RESPONSE?

Your second line of action should be the library, local bookstore, or the Internet. Request or order *The Hollywood Creative Directory's Producers*. (See page 80 for contact information.) It is updated a few times each year, but you (or your writers group) may want to consider purchasing this reference manual once a year.

When you receive your directory, read the entries carefully, noting which companies specialize in television or features. Be aware that most major studios and larger production companies have strongly enforced legal policies regarding unsolicited submissions and will usually return such material unread.

However, many successful writers have started their careers by using what I call the "backdoor method." It is a well-known fact in Hollywood that many of the smaller production companies are more flexible about accepting submissions from non-represented writers who will sign a standard release form (see page 190). Often the smaller companies will only option a project, rather than buy it outright. Still, many writers have secured an option and then asked a contact at the production company to suggest a possible agent.

If an agent knows you have proven talent (the option), he may be more open to looking at you as a potential client, especially if you let him know that you have more than one script, with several other ideas in the works. The agent, who wants to be in business with the production company, will usually take a look at your script if it is referred to him by a development exec at the company. This is part of the unwritten favor system of networking which has been in existence for decades, and a clear-cut example of how networking in the Biz pays off.

ARE THERE OTHER OPTIONS?

Other helpful publications are *The Hollywood Scriptwriter* (P.O. Box 10277, Burbank, CA 91510, (866)479-7483, *www.hollywood scriptwriter.com*) and *The New York Screenwriter* ((718)398-7197, *www.nyscreenwriter.com*). Each of these publications devotes an issue annually to agencies who are open to material from promising writers looking for representation.

Also, screenwriting groups, like the American Screenwriters Association (*www.asascreenwriters.com*), have Web sites which often list helpful links (to production companies, agencies, and even foreign production entities) that may prove useful in obtaining a sale or an option, which, in turn, could be used to interest an agency in you and your work.

WHAT DO AGENTS LOOK FOR IN CLIENTS?

Agents look for focused and determined writers. They want writers who are in for the long haul. A writer should have at least two or three scripts to show, with outlines or treatments for at least another one or two. In addition to the obvious factor of talent, agents want clients who have work that will sell, so at least one or two of your scripts should be for a mainstream audience (comedy, romance, action, adventure, family, or mystery/thriller).

This advice is not meant to stifle your creative talent, but is said with the knowledge that the more potential buyers your agent can present your screenplays to, the greater your exposure. On the other hand, a well-written script that is smaller in focus, more unusual, and not mainstream, only needs one buyer; a good agent who recognizes your gem will work diligently to find that buyer.

Agents are not much different from producers and studio execs. They, too, want fully-developed characters, strong structure, solid dialogue, with an attention-getting writing style that is generally spare but also creative, visual, and telling. As one of my favorite agents once quipped, "It's also a plus if a writer client is patient, open-minded, and flexible."

WHICH AGENCY IS BEST?
Agents and agencies are to be viewed like all business partners — with a combination of suspicion and hope. Some are ultimately better than others. However, once you have an agent, if that person turns out not to be a good fit for you, you can always part with them (if they have not found work for you after a specified timespan) and attempt to secure another agent. Some writers have managed to query the interest of other agents before actually making the split from the first agency. But this type of maneuver must be handled carefully; a less experienced writer could find himself being dropped altogether and without anyone to represent him if he is not careful.

For writers who are new in the business, it is best to start with the smaller literary agencies, the ones that are mentioned in the WGA list of agencies who are willing to look at unsolicited material.

Why not the big, splashy, headline-getting agencies who make those million-dollar deals? Most of those mega-agencies only have clients who have already established a name and a solid career for themselves by having at least one or two produced movies. Also, most of those mega-agencies focus more on packaging projects by taking a client's script and attaching a director and/or acting talent from the same agency, in order to claim fees from the writer, the director, and the actor. And more importantly, mega-agencies do not always have the time that is necessary to help an emerging writer with his struggling career.

WHAT IS AN ENTERTAINMENT ATTORNEY?

Entertainment attorneys can perform similar tasks to an agent. They will often be willing to submit material to their contacts at different production houses and studios. The biggest difference, however, is that they are not bound to the WGA. Therefore, entertainment attorneys can charge as little as 5 percent or as much as 20 percent or more if they are able to submit and sell one of your screenplays. Some attorneys will charge additional fees for negotiating contracts or submitting scripts.

If you are interested in obtaining an attorney to represent you, you will need to ask the following questions:

- How long has the attorney done business in the entertainment industry?

- Is she an independent attorney or is she part of a larger law firm?

- What is needed to hire her as your representative?

- Does she require an annual retainer or does she work on a "per project" basis?

- What will the retainer or the fee entitle you to? Will submissions cost extra? Does she charge fees for having your work messengered to the production entity? Does she charge for making copies of your script? What percentage does she charge if she submits your screenplay and it sells?

- Does she become involved in packaging a project, that is, will she take your project to the agencies to find either acting or directing talent that will sign on as part of your project? Does she charge extra for packaging?

- Is she a member of the California Bar Association (licensed to practice law in the state of California, where a majority of the entertainment industry operates)?

- Does she represent other members of the entertainment community besides other writers?

Many agents have strong ties to seasoned entertainment attorneys and many of them work hand-in-hand to represent writers as a team. Most successful writers have both an agent and an entertainment lawyer.

WHAT IS AN ENTERTAINMENT MANAGER?

Entertainment managers are not entirely new to the industry, but there seem to be more managers than ever before. Many well-known former agents (some from the mega-agencies) have set up house as entertainment managers.

Like the entertainment attorneys, the managers are not WGA-affiliated. As of this writing, there are no legal boundaries that regulate a manager, so managers can often charge higher percentages than agents. In addition, most managers will only take on clients who are already established.

What are the advantages of having a manager? Because managers usually have fewer clients than at an agency, they can often invest more time in helping to mold a writer's career. Several managers are former studio or production execs who specialize in helping writers develop their work so it is "market-ready." Agents (especially ones at the mega-agencies) usually do not have the time to make this effort.

Also, many managers who take an active interest in their writers may also want to attach themselves as producers if a client's screenplay is sold. Depending on your relationship with your manager, such an attachment can occasionally be a blessing or a curse. Some managers will also work cooperatively with clients who have agents.

DO I NEED AN ENTERTAINMENT MANAGER?
Chances are, if you are a writer who does not have a produced movie under his belt, you will not derive much benefit from employing an entertainment manager. But many career scriptwriters have managers *and* agents, as well as entertainment attorneys.

WHAT IS A SCRIPT CONSULTANT?
Where do you turn if you have finished your screenplay but would like a professional opinion of the writing quality or marketability before sending your project to an agent, a studio, or a producer? Where can you get an expert's advice on marketing yourself and your work? The answer could be: from a **scriptbuster**, otherwise known as a script consultant.

Scriptwriting and entertainment consultants were a rarity fifteen to twenty years ago, but in the past decade, a number of these consultants have emerged. For new scriptwriters, the idea of entrusting their work to the scrutiny of a consultant can be intimidating and daunting, but it can also be extremely time-worthy and cost effective.

Consultants come in all varieties. Some specialize in helping scriptwriters fine-tune their actual writing skills, while others emphasize an overall professional evaluation of a writer's work. Still others concentrate on strategies for marketing a writer and her work.

Consultants can serve an important function for emerging scriptwriters — whether Hollywood is in their backyards or not. Most new scripters do not have immediate access to direct communication with others active in the motion picture and television industries. Good consultants should know what is selling and who is looking for what.

At the same time, it is imperative for writers to understand that with such a large volume of material going over transoms, a less experienced writer may have only one shot at each studio, production house, or agency. Few agents, producers, or executives will agree to take a second look at a screenplay, even if the project has been completely revamped and revised. As a result, many scriptwriters want the assurance that each time their work is submitted, it is in the best professional form possible. Having a consultant look over a writer's work is often the best way to obtain such peace of mind.

FINDING A CONSULTANT

One way to find a script consultant is through your writers group or by personal recommendation. Talk with members in your group or with other writers who may have had the opportunity to use or hear about a screenplay specialist, and do not be afraid to query people about their experiences.

Larger literary organizations are also excellent resources for locating individuals who can give you a professional appraisal. Organizations like the American Screenwriters Association have listings of consultants who specialize in evaluating film and television projects. A careful search of such writer-friendly magazines and newsletters such as *Writer's Digest*, *The Hollywood Scriptwriter*, or *The New York Screenwriter* may turn up ads or articles on industry consultants.

Online writers chat groups can often yield other writers who have had the opportunity of hiring a scriptbuster. Words of warning: There have been a number of "consultants" who have advertised online with very low fees but are not legitimate experts. It is always advisable to check out their career backgrounds and to ask questions: How long have they been in business? Where did they train, and with whom? You might also ask for references.

If you are attending a writers conference, you might want to ask some of your fellow participants if they have worked with a competent script specialist. This is not only a great way to obtain the name of an expert, but it is also a terrific way to start a networking conversation.

SELECTING A CONSULTANT

The smart writer will immediately ascertain the credentials of any specialist. How much industry experience does the consultant have, and how current is her connection to film or television? In what capacity has this person worked in the industry (executive, story analyst, writer, producer, acquisitions specialist, agent)?

Does the consultant have experience in a specific area which applies to your project (film, television, animation, etc.)?

Has this person taught before? While the consultant you select does not have to be a certified teacher or a professor, it is often reassuring to know that the expert has experience in successfully communicating comments, ideas, and advice. Teaching experience can include workshops, seminars, and conferences.

In addition to asking for industry experience, it is important to find out what critique method is used. How detailed is the critique? Is it verbal (via a phone meeting, personal meeting, or by audio cassette)? Is the evaluation a written one? Does the consultant make notations directly on the margins of the script? Is the critique a combination of any of the above?

Another important and potentially expensive consideration is the consultant's fee. A recent query into current fees for written critiques for full-length motion picture scripts turned up amounts ranging from $250 for a two-page evaluation, to $500-$1,500 for a five-page critique with or without script notations, to a whopping $5,000 for a two-page commentary/letter. Fees also vary according to the length of the material and its type — treatment, television series proposal, story outline or synopsis, feature-length film, half-hour sitcom episode, or one-hour dramatic episode. Generally speaking, the lengthier the material, the higher the fee.

In rare cases, some screenplay specialists charge by the hour. These fees range from $25 to $250 per hour, often with a two-hour minimum.

Incidentally, most script consultants will not recommend a client's work to an agent or a producer unless the story and the writing are extraordinary. Unless a consultant tells you she would like to personally show your work to a producer, a studio, or an agent, do not assume that the consultant evaluating your project is willing to use industry connections to obtain an agent for you or seek a possible sale for your work.

KNOWING WHAT TO EXPECT

If your consultant provides a verbal critique, you can expect an oral evaluation that lasts anywhere between thirty to sixty minutes in length.

Written evaluations can run from two to thirty single-spaced pages of commentary, although most consultants seem to average between four to ten pages. Most of the comments are organized in either chronological script order (notes starting with page one and progressing in chronological order to the finish) or by major subject headings (i.e., characterization, dialogue, structure, theme, pacing, etc.).

Some consultants will make notations directly on the margins of your screenplay, thus highlighting awkward scene transitions, typos, inconsistent dialogue, pacing problems, questions of logic, etc. Many consultants combine their margin notes with either a written or an oral evaluation so a writer can readily identify the areas of concern discussed in the body of the evaluation.

Most script specialists (but not all) will also include a follow-up. Follow-ups usually take one of two forms:

- A letter answering any questions the writer may have about the critique

- A 15 to 30-minute phone call from the writer to discuss any questions the writer may have after reading the evaluation

Evaluations can be done in as short a time as a few days or may take as long as four to six weeks, depending upon how detailed an evaluation is requested. Industry consultants usually charge a higher rate if a rush is requested. Ask up front what the consultant's schedule is like. Do not wait until the last week if your goal is to submit your material to meet the deadline of a script competition or fellowship program. If, however, you are up against a time limitation, you will need to decide whether you want to pay the extra money to procure the rush services of a consultant.

Be aware that most industry specialists have other work commitments that may sometimes take precedence over a consultation (unless they are full-time consultants). On the average, it should take anywhere from two to four weeks to get a detailed, five-page evaluation of a feature script. Evaluations of treatments, outlines, or shorter pieces of work will probably take slightly less time.

SENDING YOUR SCRIPT
When sending out your script to a consultant, remember to do the following:

- Send a clean copy (not the original!) of your material. No handwritten notes or corrections, please.

- Be sure your script is on white bond, three-hole punched, and held together with brads that are long enough to secure your work. Card stock covers are optional, but highly recommended.

- All pages should be numbered and in correct sequential order. Check for any missing or duplicate pages.

- Include a cover letter that states what the material is for (i.e., a treatment for a Movie of the Week, a proposal for a sitcom, a screenplay for an animated feature film, etc.) and what the genre is (romantic comedy, suspense, action-adventure, horror, etc.). If there are specific questions or areas of concern you would like covered, be sure to mention them in your letter. It is also helpful to let the consultant know if you are planning to submit your work to an agent, a producer, or a script competition.

- While this suggestion is purely optional, you might want to include a sentence or two on how the project came to be, if you can do that briefly. It is also helpful to let the consultant know if your material is based on a book or a true-life incident.

- Enclose a SASE large enough and with sufficient postage for the return of your work. If there is a time factor involved, make arrangements for a prepaid rush delivery service (i.e., Federal Express, DHL, Express Mail, or similar services).

- Do not forget to include your check or money order for the agreed-upon fee, along with your phone number and e-mail address in case the consultant needs to ask you a question or has a scheduling delay.

READING YOUR EVALUATION

Once your material has been evaluated and returned, carefully read (and/or listen to) all the comments, suggestions, and margin notes. Then wait a day and read the evaluation again, making notations if there are areas or comments you do not agree with or understand. It is also helpful to note internally why you disagree with the consultant on a specific point. If your evaluation includes a follow-up, list your questions and comments in the order of importance, keeping any limitations in mind (e.g., a written follow-up letter should be no longer than one to one and one-half pages, and a follow-up phone call should not exceed the agreed-upon time limit).

Any and all comments made about formatting, typos, and misspellings should be heeded and corrected. While the content of your material is the primary focus, any indication that a writer is sloppy or less than totally professional can sometimes detract from the story you are trying to tell.

If your follow-up is via telephone, carefully make notes on any suggestions or advice the consultant may give. If there is time, you may want to pitch your revision to the consultant for his feedback. This is an excellent way to know if you are on the right track. After your follow-up, sit down with your calendar and make a schedule for your revision, giving yourself a realistic deadline.

Understand up front that you are paying a consultant to give you her unsolicited, unbiased evaluation. You are not paying a consultant to praise your work to the skies unless it truly warrants that praise.

WHAT AGENTS, ATTORNEYS, MANAGERS, AND CONSULTANTS CANNOT DO

While agents, attorneys, managers, and consultants can help a writer by submitting your work, negotiating your contract, and giving you a professional evaluation, your greatest ally is yourself. Agents, attorneys, managers, and consultants cannot guarantee you work, nor can they guarantee you a career. They are professionals who can help facilitate your career.

The most successful writers in the industry did not get to the top by laying back and having their cadre of agents, managers, and attorneys do their job. It is imperative that writers realize that in this business, you have to keep on top of things. Continue to network and research by bringing any interesting project-related information to the attention of your agent or manager. If you happen to meet a production exec at a party and he or she expresses an interest in seeing your work, set up a meeting and tell your agent or manager about it. By letting your agent and/or manager know what you are doing, you will assure that you are not stepping on his toes. It could be that your agent is working on getting a meeting for you with another exec at that company.

As in any other business, open communication is the key to gaining information that will help you to get ahead and forge better working relationships.

PROTECTING YOUR WORK

In addition to registering your screenplay with the Writers Guild of America, you should also consider the following advice given to me by several of my writer friends:

COPIES

Always have extra copies of your work, either paper copies or copies on disks or CDs. In general, backup disks/CDs are the best choice. If you do not have access to a computer or are computer-shy, consider having a computer-literate friend or a relative enter your material on disk/CD. In addition, there are service bureaus that do disk/CD conversions and scanning for a fee.

Never send the original of your work to anyone — send a copy only. It is amazing how many new writers will send me the original of their work. While most executives, producers, agents, and consultants are honest and reliable, it is still best to send only a copy.

Be sure your copies include all pages and that all copies are clean and legible. There is nothing more frustrating than reading a script that has missing pages. And third- or fourth-generation copies can strain the eyes (and patience) of anyone evaluating your material.

STORAGE

Invest in a fire-rated document filing box or a safety deposit box. Keep original paper copies and backup disks/CDs stored in these boxes. Fire-rated document boxes can be pricey, but they are worth the cost to ensure one's peace of mind. For $15 to $25 a year, you can rent a safety deposit box at your local bank. Check first; many of these boxes are not large enough to accommodate full-length screenplays.

In addition, keep a backup disk/CD with a trusted friend or a relative. One writer told me that he sends a copy of each completed script to his sister, who lives out of state. Some people have told him that this is a bit of an over-reaction on his part, but he claims the ground never shakes in his hometown in Iowa, and he still does not trust living on Southern California soil.

These precautions so far have addressed the physical protection of your treatments, teleplays, and screenplays. But you also need to take precautions that address the possibility of fraud, theft, or plagiarism. Remember, however, that you are protecting only your particular collection of words, not the overall idea. In fact, it has been my experience that great ideas (as opposed to actual scripts or books) are not exclusive to any one person. Given the large number of treatments and scripts submitted every year, there are relatively few valid cases of theft or plagiarism that come to court. However, all writers are wise to consider the following protection.

RELEASE FORMS

If you do not have an agent, it is imperative that you sign a release form whenever you submit a project. Simply ask the production company or the agency for a release form. If the company does not provide one, send your own. Most scriptwriters groups have access to copies of standard release forms.

While these forms provide few guarantees (except for title of work and date of submission), they can serve as additional proof if you find yourself in a legal hassle with the company or the agency. Writers, especially those trying to get their first break, should keep in mind that the production company and/or agency is doing them a favor by considering their material. Once you have an agent and/or have more industry experience under your belt, release forms will become unnecessary.

PAPER TRAIL

Consider starting a file for each project. List the date and the time of each meeting (whether in person or in an extended conference call) where you discuss or pitch one of your projects. Under each listing, note the following:

190

- Did you leave a copy of the script or the treatment or a pitch on paper?

- If so, which version?

- Who was in attendance at the meeting?

- Did anyone take notes?

- What was their reaction to the pitch?

You may want to send a note to the executive or producer, thanking him for the chance to discuss your project. This is not only common courtesy and a valuable part of networking, but it also leaves a paper trail that can refresh your memory, should it become necessary in an arbitration. Be sure to put a copy of any correspondence concerning one of your projects into your project file.

If you have an agent, call shortly after the pitch or meeting. Let your agent know how the meeting went. Note which project(s) you pitched or discussed and what the exec's or producer's reaction or attitude was. This is part of communicating with your agent and will give her an idea of how best to follow up with the exec or the producer.

While agents usually keep a written phone log and notations on their clients' meetings, most writers tell me they also keep their own project meeting files. They do this in case they ever find it necessary to change agencies or their agent moves on to another firm or a non-agent position.

With good fortune, hopefully none of you will ever experience the loss of your work to a natural disaster or an unscrupulous person. But taking some preventative measures can go a long way toward keeping any disaster from also including the demise of your work.

A FEW LAST WORDS

In my career I have had the wonderful opportunity to meet and work with thousands of writers. Some have won Oscars and Emmys, while many others were just starting on their very first script. One thing most of these people had in common was an insatiable compulsion to put words to paper with the hope of committing those words to film. And whether their latest script sold or was rejected, the writers who ultimately succeeded or continued to work were those who just could not stop writing.

Some might view these people as obsessed, but I beg to differ. True writers cannot help themselves. They are driven to write. And although writer's block does come along every once in a while, for the most part, writers cannot stop the ideas and the words from flowing — and, we, the movie-going public, are the fortunate beneficiaries of their creative insanity!

To all the wonderful writers I have worked with — past, present, and future — thank you for inspiring me with your creativity and empowering the world with your words!

ABOUT KATHIE FONG YONEDA

KATHIE FONG YONEDA has worked in film and television for over twenty-five years. She has held executive positions at Disney, Touchstone, Disney TV Animation, and Island Pictures, and is currently at Paramount Pictures as a story analyst/development specialist.

Kathie is an internationally known seminar leader on screenwriting and development and has conducted workshops in France, Germany, Austria, Spain, Ireland, Great Britain, and throughout the U.S. and Canada. She was a special guest of the Soviet Peace Committee for a symposium in Moscow and was selected Keynote Speaker for Asian-Pacific Heritage Month at the Smithsonian Institute.

Kathie also serves on the executive board of the American Screenwriters Association and is a member of CAPE (Coalition of Asian-Pacifics in Entertainment). She has been published in *Writers Aide* and *The Portable Writers Conference*, and has been interviewed for dozens of newspapers, radio segments, and television shows.

Kathie has an independent script-consulting business whose clientele includes several award-winning writers and producers. She is also the creator of *Writing For The New Millennium*, a weekend screenwriting intensive with Academy-Award winning writer, Pamela Wallace (*Witness)*.

Kathie lives in Pasadena, California, with her husband and their two cats.

THE WRITER'S JOURNEY
2nd Edition
Mythic Structure for Writers

Christopher Vogler

See why this book has become an international best-seller and a true classic. First published in 1992, *The Writer's Journey* explores the powerful relationship between mythology and storytelling in a clear, concise style that's made it required reading for movie executives, screenwriters, scholars, and fans of pop culture all over the world.

Both fiction and nonfiction writers will discover a set of useful myth-inspired storytelling paradigms (i.e., "The Hero's Journey") and step-by-step guidelines to plot and character development. Based on the work of Joseph Campbell, *The Writer's Journey* is a must for all writers interested in further developing their craft.

The updated and revised 2nd Edition provides new insights, observations, and film references from Vogler's ongoing work on mythology's influence on stories, movies, and man himself.

Christopher Vogler, a top Hollywood story consultant and development executive, has worked on such high-grossing feature films as The Lion King *and* The Thin Red Line *and conducts writing workshops around the globe.*

$24.95
Order # 98RLS
ISBN: 0-941188-70-1

THE PERFECT PITCH
How to Sell Yourself and Your Movie Idea to Hollywood

Ken Rotcop as told to James Shea

A good pitch can mean the difference between seeing your name on a lucrative studio contract or a form rejection letter. It's a well-known industry fact that film executives typically devote about two minutes of their attention to directors and screenwriters who bring them their ideas hoping for a deal. Can you capture their attention and pique their interest in the time it takes to order a latte at Starbucks? Your future as a successful screenwriter or director may depend on it.

Author Ken Rotcop writes from a unique perspective—he's made hundreds of pitches himself as a screenwriter and producer and heard many more as creative director of four studios. Using personal examples of successes and failures, Rotcop shows you how to walk the tightrope of a pitch meeting without falling off. Which attention-grabbing strategies can make a studio head put down his daily horoscope and listen to *you*? Once you've got his attention, how can you "reel him in" and get him excited about your idea? What if you forget what you were going to say? What if you make a faux pas? Does "no" always mean "no" in the language of movie deals?

Rotcop discusses these situations and others, as well as how to best present yourself and your idea, how and when to do "on-the-spot" pitching, and how to recognize and capitalize on future opportunities.

Ken Rotcop produces Pitchmart™, Hollywood's biggest screenplay pitch event.

$16.95
Order # 14RLS
ISBN: 0-941188-31-0

SCREENWRITING ON THE INTERNET
Researching, Writing, and Selling Your Script on the Web

Christopher Wehner

The Internet can save you loads of money, time and effort–but only if you know how to exploit it. *Screenwriting on the Internet* is your road map to using the information superhighway to further your screenwriting career. Packed with time- and money-saving tips, this book tells you exactly where you need to go and what you need to do to get the information you want, whether you're doing research or looking to submit your screenplay to the right agent or producer.

Includes step-by-step instructions on the do's and don'ts of e-mail querying, a definitive directory of over 300 industry e-mail addresses and Web sites, and much more.

You'll learn how you can write your script on a beach in Maui, e-mail it to partners in London, and cash your paycheck in Hollywood!

Christopher Wehner founded The Screenwriters Utopia, which has become one of the most popular and heavily visited sites for writers on the Internet.

$16.95
Order #5RLS
ISBN: 0-941188-36-1

THE WRITER'S PARTNER
1001 Breakthrough Ideas
to Stimulate Your Imagination

Martin Roth

The Writer's Partner is as reliable and indispensable as its title implies. Whether you're looking for inspiration for new plotlines and characters or need help fleshing out your characters and settings with depth and detail, this book will help you turn your script into a strong, memorable work. It's the complete source to turn to for help with whatever is lacking in your screenplay or novel.

Sections on character development, theme, conflict, crisis, and suspense-generating devices will teach you how to structure your story for maximum emotional effectiveness, *The Writer's Partner* even goes a step further than most screenwriting books: it not only helps you construct a plot, but also shows you how to add color and texture to make your story unique, give it resonance, and create a highly desirable script for producers and directors.

The book covers every major genre, from action to suspense to comedy to romance to horror. Find interesting occupations and settings for your characters, then learn how to flesh them out with realistic dialogue and authentic details. With *The Writer's Partner*, you'll feel like you're in a roomful of talented writers helping you to perfect your screenplay – and you don't have to share screen credit or split the profits!

Martin Roth wrote TV scripts and several best-selling books, including The Crime Writer's Reference Book.

$19.95
Order # 3RLS
ISBN: 0-941188-32-9

FILM DIRECTING: SHOT BY SHOT
Visualizing from Concept to Screen

Steven D. Katz

This classic with the famous blue cover is one of the most well-known books in the business, and is a favorite of working directors as an on-set quick-reference guide. Packed with visual techniques for filmmakers and screenwriters to expand their stylistic knowledge, this international best-seller contains in-depth information on composition, previsualization, camera techniques, and much more. Includes over 750 storyboards and illustrations, with never-before-published storyboards from Spielberg's *Empire of the Sun*, Welles' *Citizen Kane*, and Hitchcock's *The Birds*.

$27.95
Order # 7RLS
ISBN: 0-941188-10-8

Both Katz Books Only $47

Save 12% when you order both books
Order #KatzB

FILM DIRECTING: CINEMATIC MOTION
A Workshop for Staging Scenes

Steven D. Katz

This follow-up to the phenomenally popular *Shot by Shot* is a practical guide to common production problems encountered when staging and blocking film scenes. Includes discussions of scheduling, staging without dialogue, sequence shots, actor and camera choreography, and much more. Also includes interviews with well-known professionals such as director John Sayles and visual effects coordinator Van Ling (*The Abyss, Terminator 2*).

$24.95
Order # 6RLS
ISBN: 0-941188-14-0

DIRECTING ACTORS
*Creating Memorable Performances
for Film & Television*

Judith Weston

The most important relationship on a movie set is between director and actor. The director is responsible for telling the story and the actors are responsible for bringing the story to life. *Directing Actors* is a method for establishing creative, mutually beneficial relationships between actors and directors. Using simple, practical tools that both directors and actors can use immediately, this book will show you how to get the most out of rehearsals, troubleshoot poor performances, and give directions that are clear, succinct, and easy to follow.

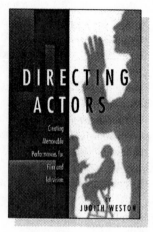

$26.95
Order # 4RLS
ISBN: 0-941188-24-8

SETTING UP YOUR SHOTS
Great Camera Moves Every Filmmaker Should Know

Jeremy Vineyard

Written in straightforward, non-technical language and laid out in a non-linear format with self-contained chapters for easy reference, *Setting Up Your Shots* is like a Swiss army knife for filmmakers! Using examples from over 140 popular films, this book provides detailed descriptions of more than 100 camera setups, angles, and techniques. An excellent primer for beginning filmmakers and

students of film theory, as well as a handy quick-reference guide for working filmmakers.

Contains 150 references to the great shots in your favorite films, including *2001: A Space Odyssey, Blue Velvet, The Matrix, The Usual Suspects, Vertigo* and more.

$19.95, Order # 8RLS, ISBN: 0-941188-73-6

INDEPENDENT FILM & VIDEOMAKER'S GUIDE
2nd Edition
Expanded & Updated

Michael Wiese

The new, completely expanded and revised edition of one of our best-sellers has all the information you need, from fundraising to distribution. This practical and comprehensive book will help filmmakers save time and **money** and inspire them to create successful projects.

Contents include:

- Writing a business plan
- Developing your ideas into concepts, treatments, and scripts
- Directing, producing, and market research
- Understanding distribution markets (theatrical, home video, television, international)
- Financing your film
- Making presentations and writing a prospectus

Plus, an appendix filled with film cash flow projections, sample contracts, valuable contact addresses, and much more.

Using the principles outlined in this book, Wiese recently co-directed the short film *Field of Fish*, and is currently preparing his Bali feature. Additionally, Wiese is national spokesperson for Kodak's Emerging Filmmakers Program. He has conducted workshops on independent filmmaking in England, Germany, Finland, Indonesia, Ireland, Canada, Australia, and throughout the U.S. Contact Wiese at mw@mwp.com.

$29.95
Order # 37RLS
ISBN: 0-941188-57-4

ORDER FORM

TO ORDER THESE PRODUCTS, PLEASE CALL **24** HOURS - **7** DAYS A WEEK
CREDIT CARD ORDERS **1-800-833-5738** OR FAX YOUR ORDER **(818) 986-3408**
OR MAIL THIS ORDER FORM TO:

MICHAEL WIESE PRODUCTIONS
11288 VENTURA BLVD., # 621
STUDIO CITY, CA 91604
E-MAIL: MWPSALES@MWP.COM
WEB SITE: WWW.MWP.COM

WRITE OR FAX FOR A FREE CATALOG

PLEASE SEND ME THE FOLLOWING BOOKS:

TITLE	ORDER NUMBER (#RLS ____)	AMOUNT
_____	_____	_____
_____	_____	_____
_____	_____	_____
_____	_____	_____
_____	_____	_____
	SHIPPING	_____
	CALIFORNIA TAX (8.00%)	_____
	TOTAL ENCLOSED	_____

SHIPPING:
ALL ORDERS MUST BE PREPAID, UPS GROUND SERVICE ONE ITEM - **$3.95**
EACH ADDITIONAL ITEM ADD **$2.00**
EXPRESS - **3** BUSINESS DAYS ADD **$12.00** PER ORDER
OVERSEAS
SURFACE - **$15.00** EACH ITEM   AIRMAIL - **$30.00** EACH ITEM

PLEASE MAKE CHECK OR MONEY ORDER PAYABLE TO:

MICHAEL WIESE PRODUCTIONS

(CHECK ONE) ____ MASTERCARD ____ VISA ____ AMEX

CREDIT CARD NUMBER _____

EXPIRATION DATE _____

CARDHOLDER'S NAME _____

CARDHOLDER'S SIGNATURE _____

SHIP TO:

NAME _____

ADDRESS _____

CITY _____ STATE _____ ZIP _____

COUNTRY _____ TELEPHONE _____

ORDER ONLINE FOR THE LOWEST PRICES

24 HOURS | 1.800.833.5738 | www.mwp.com